Administration of
Special Education

ADMINISTRATION OF SPECIAL EDUCATION

A Guide for General Administrators and Special Educators

By

B. R. GEARHEART, Ed.D.

Associate Professor of Special Education
Colorado State College
Greeley, Colorado

CHARLES C THOMAS · PUBLISHER
Springfield · Illinois · U.S.A.

Published and Distributed Throughout the World by

CHARLES C THOMAS • PUBLISHER

BANNERTONE HOUSE

301-327 East Lawrence Avenue, Springfield, Illinois, U.S.A.

NATCHEZ PLANTATION HOUSE

735 North Atlantic Boulevard, Fort Lauderdale, Florida, U.S.A.

© *1967, by* CHARLES C THOMAS • PUBLISHER

Library of Congress Catalog Card Number: 67-25708

With THOMAS BOOKS *careful attention is given to all details of
manufacturing and design. It is the Publisher's desire to present books
that are satisfactory as to their physical qualities and artistic possibilities
and appropriate for their particular use.* THOMAS BOOKS *will be true
to those laws of quality that assure a good name and good will.*

Printed in the United States of America

C-1

Preface

ONE of the first references in which the term "Special Education" was used was in a speech given by Dr. Alexander Graham Bell to the National Education Association convention in 1902. To understand fully his usage of the term at this convention, we must refer to his closing address at the N. E. A. meeting in 1898. In this address he pointed out the need for special instruction for exceptional children in these words:

> Now, all that I have said in relation to the deaf would be equally advantageous to the blind and to the feeble-minded. We have in the public school system a large body of ordinary children in the same community. We have there children who cannot hear sufficiently well to profit by instruction in the public schools, and we have children who cannot see sufficiently well to profit by instruction in the public schools, and we have children who are undoubtedly backward in their mental development. Why shouldn't these children form an annex to the public school system, receiving special instruction from special teachers, who shall be able to give instruction to little children who are either deaf, blind, or mentally deficient, without sending them away from their homes or from the ordinary companions with whom they are associated?

Then, in 1902, Dr. Bell pursued this subject further, and as a result the name of this division of the N. E. A. officially became the "Department of Special Education."

Since that time, programs of special education have developed in public school systems, both large and small, throughout the United States.

The administration of these programs was at first a direct responsibility of the superintendent of schools, with no director, supervisor, or consultant appearing in the line of command between the superintendent and the classroom teacher. Today, most medium-sized and large school systems employ a director to administer and supervise the special education program. A relatively new development is the cooperative district, which may coordinate special education services for many "regular" school districts of smaller size.

There is mounting evidence that those who administer a program of special education must be well-informed regarding the regular school program, must have considerable knowledge in the various areas of exceptionality served by the special education program, and must be well-trained, competent administrators as well. Both the general administrator (the superintendent of schools) and the special education administrator are in need of a guide or handbook designed to cover comprehensively the area of administration of special education. This text has been designed to help fill the need.

Acknowledgments

MUCH credit, and my personal thanks go to Edward Meyen for his major contribution to this text, and to Dr. Daniel McAlees for ideas relative to the role of vocational rehabilitation. Also, a word of appreciation is due Dr. Tony Vaughan for encouragement to enter the field of special education.

B. R. GEARHEART

Contents

Administration of Special Education

I
Special Education—Then and Now

SPECIAL EDUCATION for exceptional boys and girls is now an accepted part of the American public school system, but prior to 1900, nearly all school programs for handicapped or gifted children were private in nature. During the period from 1900 to 1930, public school classes for exceptional children grew quite rapidly, but the most remarkable growth has been since 1930. By 1967, a large majority of school systems in the United States provided some type of special education services and well over a million children and young people were being served by such programs.

Various factors have contributed to the growth of special education in the United States. The rapid numerical growth of our entire educational system (with corresponding numerical growth in the number of exceptional children) has played a role.

The fact that handicapped boys and girls are not kept hidden in attics and cellars has been another factor. Probably the most important single factor is the growth of the philosophy of "education for all," and the resultant inclusion of most of the various handicapping conditions.

Various exceptionalities have received special attention during certain periods of time in the past sixty years, but none has had greater attention than is now being given to the mentally retarded. Our late president, John F. Kennedy, in a formal statement on October 11, 1961, outlined the tremendous need in this area. The opening words in his statement exemplify the type of emphasis which our society periodically places on one handicap or another. The president said:

> The manner in which our nation cares for its citizens and conserves its manpower resources is more than an index to its concern for the less fortunate. It is a key to its future. Both wisdom and humanity dictate a deep interest in the physically handicapped, the mentally ill, and the mentally retarded. Yet, although we have made con-

3

siderable progress in the treatment of physical handicaps, although we have attacked on a broad front the problems of mental illness, although we have made great strides in the battle against disease, we as a nation have too long postponed an intensive search for solutions to the problems of the mentally retarded. That failure should be corrected.

In discussing the scope of the problem, the president pointed out that approximately five million persons in our country are retarded, and at the present rate another one million retarded children will be on the scene by 1970.

In terms of national welfare, over 700,000 draftees were unfit for service during World War II because of mental retardation or illiteracy; many of the illiterate were simply retarded.

The financial load to local communities for the 3 to 4 per cent of the mentally retarded who are institutionalized is approximately three hundred million dollars annually; but the financial load through unemployment benefits, confinement in penal or correctional institutions and other less obvious costs for the other 96 or 97 per cent is even more staggering. Through improper or insufficient educational opportunities, unrealistic employment conditions, and public treatment and reaction based on prejudice and misinformation, the mentally retarded individual literally does not have a chance.

This same rationale—on a lesser scale—may be applied to all handicapping conditions.

WORLDWIDE DEVELOPMENT OF SPECIAL SCHOOL PROGRAMS FOR THE HANDICAPPED

The Blind

In 1784, the first school for the blind, *L'Institution Nationale des Jeunes Aveugles,* was founded by Valentin Hauy in Paris, France. In 1791, a school was established in Liverpool, England, followed by several others in the next twenty years. In Austria, a school was formed by Johann Wilhelm Klein in 1804, and in Berlin the Royal Institution for the Blind was founded in 1806.

The first specially printed, embossed book for the blind was produced in Paris in 1786, and was the early cousin of the Braille point alphabet, developed by Louis Braille in 1925.

Early schools for the blind were supported by private funds and many were charitable institutions. Support of these schools has been gradually taken over by city, state, and national governments.

The American Printing House for the Blind is a federally-supported institution in the United States, and has counterparts in most European countries.

In the United States, the first blind child was admitted to public education (day school) classes in Chicago in 1900. As reported by a recent Office of Education publication, there have been more marked increases in public school enrollments of the blind than any other exceptionality. During the 1948-58 decade there was a 400 per cent increase in special public school classes for the blind.

This is not due to an increase in the incidence of blindness in school-age children but, rather, reflects a trend toward public school placement rather than institutional placement for the blind child.

The Deaf

Historically, the deaf have suffered more mistreatment through lack of understanding than any other area of exceptionality. Because deaf children could not hear language, they did not learn to speak. Therefore, they were thought to be incapable of speech. Aristotle, because he felt the deaf could not speak, concluded that they were uneducable. This became the opinion of the church, and the authority of the church discouraged any other point of view for nearly two thousand years. It is reported that in the seventh century A.D., Bishop John of York taught a "deaf and dumb" boy to speak intelligently. However, this was seen as a miracle and did little to dispel the belief that a deaf person simply was incapable of speech.

In the sixteenth century, a Spanish monk, Pedro Ponce de Leon, successfully taught several deaf Spaniards of noble birth to speak. The long held theories of Aristotle were then discarded. In 1760, the *Abbé* de l'Epee opened a school for the deaf in Paris. He used a combination of oral and manual methods. A German, Samuel Heinicke, established a school for the deaf in Leipzig in 1778. He strongly advocated the oral method, as did those who originated schools for the deaf in England.

The first fruitful work in the United States on behalf of education for the deaf was done by Thomas Hopkins Galludet who founded a school in Hartford, Connecticut, in 1817. He was a follower of l'Epee, and did much to train teachers who soon established other schools in other states.

In the United States, the first and only College for the Deaf was opened in 1864; first called the National Deaf-Mute College, it was later renamed Galludet College.

About 1850, a very heated debate developed over the merits of the oral and the manual methods of teaching the deaf. Finally, in 1890, at the Convention of the American Instructors of the Deaf, an organization called the American Association to Promote the Teaching of Speech to the Deaf, was formed. Dr. Alexander Graham Bell was its first president; the oral-manual battle had been finally won by the oralists.

Today, most deaf children are being taught by the oral method, although as recently as 1950 there were many state schools for the deaf where both methods were employed.

Recent enrollment data reflects a steady increase in enrollments in public school classes for the deaf. In most states, the population in state residential schools tends to have a higher proportion of older persons each succeeding year, thus clearly indicating the trend in this area of exceptionality.

The Mentally Retarded

Historically, the mentally retarded have been viewed as a "burden" to society. In early tribal records we find evidence that mentally retarded children were often left in the wilderness to die. The Spartans destroyed such individuals in the name of preservation of the race. In the early part of this century there is evidence that midwives often made it a practice to smother defective babies before the mother had even seen them; a recent newspaper article relates a practice among present day South American Indians of throwing defective babies off a high cliff.

During the early Christian era in Rome, the mentally retarded were "saved" to serve as court jesters; following the fall of Rome there was a period of time in which the mentally retarded were "protected" and encouraged to roam as professional beggars. A similar practice was followed by the American Indians, who saw such individuals as "Sons and Daughters of the Great Spirit."

Because of religious beliefs, the mentally retarded and mentally ill suffered great persecution during the Reformation. Both the early Protestants and the Catholics believed that many mentally ill and mentally retarded were witches. It has been estimated nearly 100,000 died as witches during the two hundred-year period from the middle fifteenth to the middle seventeenth century.

One of several exceptions to this poor treatment was a shelter for feebleminded begun by St. Vincent de Paul in the early seventeenth century.

It was not until 1798 that any really significant event occurred relating to actually *teaching* the mental defective. It was then that the now-famous "Wild Boy of Aveyron" was discovered living in the woods of southern France. In Paris, Jean Itard began an attempt to teach this "wild boy," feeling that he was of normal intellectual endowment, but simply wild and untaught. After much discouragement, Itard gave up and the boy was probably institutionalized. Others at the Paris Academy of Science prevailed upon him to record his experience. They, in turn, had some effect on Edouard Seguin, who founded a school for mentally retarded in 1837. (In 1816 a school for mentally retarded was opened in Salzburg, Austria, but it closed in 1835 because of lack of success.)

Seguin came to the United States in 1848 and played a role in the establishment of several state institutions in this country; he is therefore recognized by many as the founder of present-day educational programs for the mentally retarded. In 1848, a state institutional school for mentally retarded was opened in Boston, Massachusetts.

The forerunner of our present special education classes for mentally retarded was a special class initiated for a city school system in Germany in 1867. Norway opened a similar class in 1874, with England, Austria, and Switzerland soon following.

Providence, Rhode Island, had the first public school classes for mentally retarded in 1893, followed by many other cities in the eastern United States.

A recent special education survey conducted by the U. S. Office of Education listed nearly 300,000 pupils enrolled in public school classes for the mentally retarded. Other studies have indicated an average class size of approximately fifteen students, which indicates that special public school classes for the mentally retarded have grown from one class, in 1893, to 20,000 classes by the mid-1960's.

Orthopedically Handicapped

The first specially built, or adapted school for crippled children and youth was founded by Kurtz in Munich, Germany. Originally a private institution, it was later taken over by the state. The school, residential in nature, was highly successful in preparing pupils to obtain employment after completion of training.

In England, the London school board first adopted a tax-supported school program for crippled children in 1898. One year later, the Chicago Public Schools established a special school for crippled children.

The first institution in the United States to employ teachers for crippled children was the Knight Hospital for the Ruptured and Crippled, started in New York in 1861.

A variety of programs for crippled or orthopedically handicapped may be found in the United States today, but the most significant fact about such programs is that they are not even increasing at the same rate as the total public school enrollment. Of the nine areas of exceptionality reported by the U. S. Office of Education in a recent enrollment comparison, only this type showed no increase. It is possible this is due to an increasing trend to provide for many more of these children in regular classes, rather than a significant decrease in orthopedic handicaps.

Other Exceptionalities

The historical development of other areas of exceptionality either parallel some of those already mentioned or present little of general historical interest.

School programs for the partially seeing and the hard-of-hearing have been related rather closely to those for the blind and the deaf in the past, but are now becoming more separate. With the advent of highly effective transistorized hearing aids, many hard-of-hearing pupils are able to attend regular classes with minimal help in language development and/or speech reading. Partially sighted boys and girls often function quite well in a regular classroom with large print books or pedestal-mounted magnifying devices which permit use of the same materials as other pupils.

The group which is called socially and emotionally maladjusted is the subject of considerable attention at present. A real problem here is that authorities in the field are some times at a loss after diagnosis has been completed. This is an area which will bear watching in the coming ten to twenty years.

The mentally gifted are also the center of some controversy. Since most experts in the field agree that present methods of psychometric measurement give a reliable estimate of only one dimension of intelligence, many educators feel we should wait before planning a revised instructional program for those presently classified as mentally gifted. There is also a serious question among a large number of those in general educational administration as to whether this group should fall within the realm of special education. This decision, when finally reached, may have a considerable effect on how the program for mentally gifted will develop. During a recent ten-year period the number of pupils enrolled in special classes for mentally gifted increased in the same ratio as those for mentally retarded.

The school program for children with speech impairments, commonly called speech correction or speech therapy, involves approximately one-half of the total number of children served by special education programs. This assistance in proper speech development—generally given during the elementary school years —has become increasingly popular and well-accepted since about 1930. Research relating to such serious speech disorders as stuttering has a longer history, but the major portion of the speech therapist's time goes for less serious articulation problems. With many children, a year or two of speech help on a twice-per-week basis is all that is needed. Speech improvement work in kindergarten and first grade is a more recent practice which holds considerable promise.

RECENT TRENDS IN THE UNITED STATES

In the preface to the 1963 publication, *Behavioral Research on Exceptional Children,* editors Samuel A. Kirk and Bluma B. Weiner comment as follows:

> During the past two decades, the field of special education has undergone an "explosion" both in services and in knowledge. The development of programs for exceptional children, particularly since World War II, has been so rapid that few professional workers have been able to keep up with the expanding scene. Because of the heterogeneity of this field, which includes so many kinds of deviant development, and because of the multiplicity of disciplines concerned with services and research, information processing has broken down.
>
> Much of the early literature on exceptional children pertained to physiological aspects of disability. Valuable as these findings were, there was little in them which had direct relevance to problems of school learning and social adjustment. With more recent advances in theories of perception, learning, and personality, there has emerged greater interest in, and a greater need for, information bearing upon the *behavioral* aspects of exceptionality. Responsible instruction, program development, and guidance depend upon such knowledge.

This text by the Council on Exceptional Children is organized into twelve sections or chapters. The chapter titles are: The Gifted; The Educable Mentally Retarded; The Trainable Mentally Retarded; The Visually Impaired; The Hard-of-Hearing; The Deaf; Children with Cerebral Dysfunction; Children with Orthopedic Handicaps and Special Health Problems; Children with Speech and Language Impairments; The Emotionally Disturbed; The Delinquent, and Administration.

One of the two studies reviewed under the chapter "Problem Areas" is a 1960 study conducted by the Los Angeles City Schools. This study included an attempt to determine which exceptionalities should be included under the general title, "Special Education." Those "experts" consulted included the special education personnel from thirty-nine of the fifty states and from the U. S. Office of Education, fifty-eight professors of school administration, and eighteen special education experts. This exceptionally well-constructed study resulted in substantial agreement that blind, partially seeing, deaf, hard-of-hearing, lip reading, speech correction, cerebral palsied, orthopedically handicapped, mentally retarded (educable), emotionally and socially disturbed, hospital teaching, and home teaching categories should be included as a part of special education. It was also agreed that remedial reading, remedial arithmetic, foreign adjustment classes and corrective physical education should *not* be included.

The category "mentally deficient" (trainable mentally retarded) was indicated as appropriate for inclusion in the general term "special education" by less than 60 per cent of the total group participating in the study. Thirty-three of the professors of school administration, 28 per cent of the special education specialists, and 25 per cent of the special education personnel in state departments indicated this category should *not* be included within the definition of special education.

The "gifted" category was one which elicited responses along well-defined "party lines." Ninety-four per cent of the special education specialists felt this category should be a part of their field. (There were no negative responses from this group.) From state departments, 78 per cent of the personnel felt the "gifted" should be included in the term "special education," while only 12 per cent gave a negative response.

Professors of school administration presented a different picture, with 47 per cent in favor and 43 per cent opposed to defining the "gifted" as a part of special education.

There was some disagreement as to whether or not certain areas which might be classed as special education should be included in that department of a public school. Here again, the professors of school administration replied in a manner significantly different from the other two groups. The gifted and the mentally deficient were the two groups which they felt should *not* be a part of a public school department of special education. Indications were that the mentally deficient are not necessarily a public school responsibility, and that the gifted did not belong within a public school department of special education.

It is quite significant that of the three groups of respondents to the questionnaire, only one, the state department personnel, believed the mentally deficient should be the direct responsibility of the school district.

The Los Angeles study (which is probably the best of its kind to date) also investigated the opinions of the authorities regarding five different organizational plans. These plans were labeled the "Segregated Plan," "Partial Segregation," the "Cooperative Plan," the "Resource Room" and the "Itinerant Teacher."

The type of pupil organization utilized for each exceptionality may have a great bearing on the success of that particular program of education, so it is obvious that some sort of general philosophy regarding school organization, plus specific recommendations for each exceptionality, are highly important. For purposes of this study, these organizational plans were defined as follows:

Segregated Plan: Special classes or a school not on the same site as regular school.

Partial Segregation: A section of regular school reserved for special education, or special education on the same site as regular school. No plan to specifically integrate children with "regular" classroom activities. Partial integration recognized by attendance at school assemblies, events, lunch room, or where feasible.

Cooperative Plan: Special education class or classes in which pupil may spend some portion of the day in the regular classroom.

Resource Room: Pupil is registered in regular classroom, does all his work with the regular group and goes to the resource room and the special education teacher only for materials and special training.

Itinerant Teacher: Pupil registered in regular classroom, does all his work with the regular classroom teacher, and receives periodic specialized training, help and materials from a traveling special education teacher.

The general philosophy to which a growing number of special educators ascribe might be summarized as minimal segregation, consistent with efficient education. From this point of view, the resource room or itinerant teacher would seem to be the best answer, all other conditions being equal. In practice, we find that

COMPARATIVE ANALYSIS OF PUPIL ORGANIZATION RECEIVING HIGHEST FREQUENCY

		TYPE OF ORGANIZATION THAT RECEIVED THE HIGHEST FREQUENCY		
		State Departments of Education	Special Education Experts	Professors of School Administration
DEAF	Elementary	Partial Segregation	Partial Segregation	Partial Segregation
	Secondary	Cooperative	Cooperative	Cooperative
HARD-OF-HEARING	Elementary	Cooperative	Resource Room	Cooperative
	Secondary	Resource	Resource and Itinerant	Cooperative
BLIND	Elementary	Cooperative	Partially Segregated	Segregated
	Secondary	Resource	Resource Room	Seg.; P. Seg.; Co-op.
PARTIALLY SEEING	Elementary	Cooperative	Resource Room	Cooperative
	Secondary	Resource and Itinerant	Resource Room	Cooperative
EMOTIONALLY AND SOCIALLY DISTURBED	Elementary	Partial Segregation	Partially Segregated	Cooperative
	Secondary	Cooperative	Partially Segregated	Cooperative
CRIPPLED	Elementary	Cooperative	Partially Segregated	Cooperative
	Secondary	Cooperative	Cooperative	Cooperative
MENTALLY RETARDED	Elementary	Partial Segregation	Partially Segregated	Partial Segregation
	Secondary	P. Seg. and Cooperative	Cooperative	Partial Segregation
MENTALLY DEFICIENT	Elementary	Segregated	Segregated	Segregation
	Secondary	Segregated	Segregated	Segregation
CHRONIC MEDICAL PROBLEMS	Elementary	Cooperative	Cooperative	Cooperative
	Secondary	Cooperative	Cooperative	Cooperative

all other factors never are "equal," and therefore a variety of pupil organization plans are required, depending on the exceptionality. It also must be recognized that two other major factors, plus a host of minor ones, are in operation; these major requirements are money and existing plant facilities. Since new plant facilities could be provided if money were no problem, it is perhaps more realistic to say simply that the *one major factor* operating to modify what would be philosophically most desirable is money.

A composite analysis of the pupil organization plans favored by the three groups of respondents is presented in the table on page 13, taken from the Los Angeles Special Education Study.

It is encouraging to see that there is a fair degree of agreement, at least in the underlying philosophy of these responses.

An excellent summary of current concerns, interests, and trends in special education may be found by examining the official program of any recent national convention of the Council for Exceptional Children. At these national conventions, section meetings are established to discuss problems suggested by special education leadership as vital, interesting or critical. It is interesting to note that recent international meetings of the CEC (the one professional group in the United States which includes all phases of special education) seem to indicate rapidly-increasing interest in the culturally different (or deprived) child; the socially and emotionally maladjusted; general administrative problems; teacher training problems; certain specific reading disabilities, and cerebral dysfunction or the minimally brain-injured. These phases of special education, plus continued concern with improvement of quality of the "older" phases, might be considered as the major interests of special education today.

II

The Present Scope of Special Education

EXCEPTIONALITIES SERVED BY SPECIAL EDUCATION

THE mentally retarded group is probably the largest one served through special education services in the public school. Some might take exception to this in that a greater number of children may be contacted by the teacher of the speech handicapped (speech therapist). But since this is usually remedial-type instruction, and the teacher of the speech handicapped is often an itinerant teacher, the mentally retarded section is usually considered the largest served by a program of special education. Generally speaking, the mentally retarded are considered as those whose IQ is below 80; for practical purposes it may be assumed that 2 to 3 per cent of the total school population will fall into this category. Most states subdivide this group into two categories: first, the educable mentally retarded (IQ of 50 to 80) and second, the trainable mentally retarded (IQ below 50 but responsive enough to training to respond to small group instruction). There is some disagreement among educators as to whether the trainable mentally retarded child is the responsibility of public education, but present trends in state legislation seem to be going in a direction which will ultimately place this group in the hands of educators in general, and special education specifically.

The Educable Mentally Retarded

Educable mentally retarded pupils may make minimal adjustment to regular classes but almost always become drop-outs due to lack of interest in a school program which permits no real chance for success. This group represents one of the waste products of the system of the mass education which we revere so highly. For the mentally retarded, equality of opportunity may

15

mean only a chance to be exposed to a school program which is appropriate for children of considerably greater ability. These children are often not recognized for what they are. In appearance they may not be too different from the normal child. In interests they are very nearly the same as the normal child. Often they develop a verbal ability which disguises their lack of ability to learn at a normal rate in the normal school situation. They may cover up their scholastic inadequacy by "showing off" and receiving substitute recognition by their nonconformance and antisocial behavior.

It is too often said, "But they are learning in the regular classroom—why not leave them with their friends?" What is overlooked is the rate of learning and the question of the self-concept being developed. There is considerable evidence that these educable mentally retarded children need different materials, different teaching methods, and perhaps even a modified set of educational goals as the bases upon which their school program is planned.

In recent years, great strides have been made in developing curriculum materials for the educable mentally retarded. It has been recognized that although these children may not progress much further than third, fourth, or fifth grade level in reading and arithmetic skills, the traditional reading and arithmetic programs at the third through fifth grade level do not include concepts appropriate for fifteen through seventeen-year-old boys and girls. Also, the programs structured for the eight-to-ten year olds do not qualify as proper terminal programs for boys preparing to enter the work-world, or girls preparing for marriage and motherhood.

This means that arithmetic programs must be constructed which utilize arithmetic skills at the third and fourth grade level, but which present concepts related to insurance, social security, taxes, buying on time, using a checking account, and similar practical needs of the young adult. Reading and language arts programs must be devised using a minimal basic vocabulary, but must also present the critical words needed (for example) to apply for a job, read and understand want ads and to read and be able to follow traffic signs.

These needs represent a real challenge to a relatively small number of individuals engaged in such curriculum building, but present efforts indicate many better things to come.

One of the major points to remember regarding the retarded child is that he handles concrete words and concepts much better than abstract ones. It is extremely important to build his school program on real experiences, and to attempt to integrate learning into units of experience whenever possible. For example, a unit of study based on the telephone gives ample opportunity for reading experience (student-originated work); number practice (the pay telephone, telephone bills, change making); social concepts (telephone manners); understanding of the emergency help available from the fire department, police department, and many other possibilities. In most parts of the country, the telephone company will provide actual telephones for practice sessions and old telephone directories which may be used to learn practical application of alphabetizing, use of the city map, how to find emergency information, and other useful skills or concepts.

This is just one example of ways in which familiar objects or experiences may be used as vehicles for teaching the mentally retarded.

In addition to mental handicaps, there is sufficient, positive evidence that the mentally retarded child is also retarded in motor skill development. This is particularly bad when the type of employment available to these individuals is considered. One of the tasks of special education is to discover methods of promoting motor skill development so that this handicap will not place the educable mentally retarded youth at a further disadvantage when seeking employment.

There are two philosophical points of view on housing classes for the educable retarded. Some special educators seem to feel that a single school (or schools) containing only classes for the mentally retarded represents the best procedure. Others feel that these children are not different enough to be segregated to this extent, and therefore should be housed in a school building with regular classes. Both ideas have merit; but often local conditions other than educational philosophy decide this matter. The problem of housing will be discussed more adequately in another section of this text.

The Trainable Mentally Retarded

The trainable mentally retarded may be defined in general as mentally defective children who probably will not be able to be self-supporting, or even be able to provide complete self-care upon reaching physical maturity. Generally, these are children whose IQ is below 50, but obviously there may be individuals with IQ's of up to 60, or even 70, whose performance would qualify them as trainable if we accept this definition.

It follows, then, that these individuals, upon reaching maturity, will be in an institution (public or private), will be cared for by a willing and able relative or perhaps may already be living with a relative and participating in a sheltered workshop situation. In any event, their needs and the goals of their training program are considerably different from those of the educable mentally retarded. Some trainable boys and girls learn to recognize and write a number of words, can repeat their name, address and telephone number, and run errands for their parents. They may also learn to help around the home by washing dishes, answering the telephone, or doing housework. If they show promise of the potential to do these things, then these should become the goals of their school program. It is doubtful that many trainable boys and girls gain much from association with children in regular classes, so it is not as important to hold the special classes in a school building. On the other hand, this should not be an excuse for providing substandard, dark, unpleasant surroundings. A simulated home situation providing a place to learn home duties is most desirable. A small home with living room, kitchen, bedroom, and bath would be ideal. Obviously, this kind of program might be well provided through joint efforts of the school and other community agencies. This is an area where the role of the school, charitable community services and the state institutions must be spelled out so as to provide a program which is satisfactory for the retarded individual, financially feasible as possible, and emotionally and psychologically satisfactory to the parents of the retardate.

A number of studies are underway which may shed light on the outcomes of various types of programs for trainable boys and girls. Perhaps when all the information is available, more concrete, meaningful planning can be accomplished.

The Gifted

The mentally superior, or "gifted" child has been the subject of much discussion in very recent years. When the USSR sent the first satellite into orbit, a mild hysteria gripped certain sections of the American public. This hysteria was related to the belief that somehow we were overlooking our able students. In this case, the motivation was not where it properly should have been—that is, related to the student's welfare; it was not related to the overall welfare of humanity or even of the United States. Rather, it related to the belief that we were not encouraging able students to enter the fields of mathematics, engineering, physical science and those areas relating to rocketry. Since then, a more sober look at the manner in which we educate our talented or gifted children has given rise to a more educationally sound concern over the general (educational) welfare of boys and girls with a measured IQ in excess of 135 or 140. There is no complete agreement as to the point on the IQ scale at which giftedness begins but it is generally agreed to be somewhere between 135 and 140. It must be recognized that the two most-used individual tests of intelligence (Stanford-Binet and Wechsler) test only one facet of intelligence. There is much concern among educators and educational psychologists as to whether this type of capacity to perform, or the qualities and/or characteristics presently under study under the general term of creativity, are the most important, but most school programs for the mentally superior or gifted are for students with high IQ scores.

Since high IQ usually means considerable ability to handle abstract ideas, to think logically, to generalize effectively and therefore to *learn basic school subjects quickly,* these pupils will often be quite noticeable in the ordinary classroom. It is true enough that some gifted boys may become the classroom "menace," but this is the exception rather than the rule. Usually these bright pupils learn so quickly they are a problem for the teacher to keep busy. Two common solutions are "acceleration" and more "busy work." The former may be useful if used wisely, but has many shortcomings. "Busy work" is worse than permitting the gifted child to daydream. Daydreams are at least pleasant, and not a source of negative attitudes toward school and the learning process.

A third notion for these gifted boys and girls (who are usually also high achievers) is the "enrichment" concept. This has values which may commend it in many cases, but very often the regular classroom teacher is too involved with twenty-nine other pupils to make enrichment really workable. The alternative is to segregate the gifted pupils, at least for certain academic areas. It should be noted that (for example) separation of pupils who take business math in high school from pupils who take trigonometry, has been generally accepted. Some authorities would contend that separation of the gifted from pupils of average capability makes as much or more sense than the other groupings we believe are proper in public schooling.

It is the opinion of the writer that segregation of the gifted is only right and proper *if* we really do something different and more challenging with them after we segregate them. It should be remembered that there is *not* common agreement among educators that the gifted should be included as a part of special education.

The Aurally Handicapped: Deaf and Hard-of-Hearing

The deaf child is the most difficult to teach of the various single handicapping conditions usually included in a public school program of special education. A common-sense definition of the deaf would be those children who (even with the most powerful hearing aids) cannot hear well enough to understand what their more normal peers are saying in day-to-day conversation. In other words, the world of language going on about them never reaches their conscious recognition. These children must be taught to speak, and for them to be able to function successfully in a public school setting, much preschool work must be accomplished. In some states this preschool program is a part of the public schools, and in others it must be accomplished through charitable organizations—usually those supported by community service funds.

The hard-of-hearing come in all degrees, and thus also come with varying needs for special assistance. Usually, the hard-of-hearing in a special education program are those who have need for a battery-powered hearing device, and usually, there are related language problems. If a pupil can hear at a normal level through use of a hearing aid, and has well-developed language, there is no reason for placement in any type of special program. Many hard-of-hearing children have a language problem which is really the most serious educational ramification of their hearing handicap. Since reading, spelling, and in fact, the entire language arts area, are so closely related to hearing and speaking the language correctly, a common program for hard-of-hearing children is one which permits them to remain in their regular classrooms for much of the day, but go to a resource room for special help for thirty minutes to an hour each day. The amount and type of help depends on individual pupil needs.

The Visually Handicapped: Blind and Partially Sighted

The blind are those who have no vision and cannot learn through the sense of sight.

The partially sighted are those who have sufficient sight to learn (in varying degrees) through this sense. They vary from those who read easily with low power magnifying devices, to those who must struggle, even with higher powered magnification. It is obvious that the level of intellectual functioning of the blind and partially sighted, and the kind of preschool education or experience they have, are of utmost importance. Many a bright, visually handicapped child has made excellent progress in a regular classroom with a teacher who is willing to expend a small amount of additional effort and energy. Though the general public tends to think of blindness as a more serious handicap than deafness (and in some respects it is), the educational process is easier with the totally blind than with the profoundly deaf.

Orthopedically Handicapped

The orthopedically handicapped child has sometimes been the victim of overzealous special educators. If a child must walk with crutches and braces, the school may have to make some minor schedule adjustments or provide slightly different classroom furniture, but the child should stay in regular classes if at all possible. Often the job of special education is to make certain the necessary adjustments are made, and that teachers see the need for a particular child's regular class attendance. All too frequently, the school has placed such a child in a special facility, away from his peer group, and then has bragged about the "wonderful program for crippled children." Certainly some orthopedically handicapped children need a separate school program in a modified school facility, but this area of special education requires constant critical surveillance.

Speech Handicapped

A relatively large number of boys and girls reach kindergarten age with some sort of speech handicap. Many of these apparent handicaps may be nothing more than "baby-talk," and proper speech improvement techniques on the part of the kindergarten teacher may work wonders. But for those children who still have defective speech after a full year of kindergarten, a program of speech correction is vital. Most of these boys and girls do nothing more serious than make articulation errors, but these can prove a real handicap, particularly as they relate to learning in the all-important language arts area. These children can be helped through a good program of speech correction. Some speech handicaps are a direct result of hearing deficits, in which case a carefully coordinated program is required.

Lowered Vitality (Fragile)

Children included in this category are those with heart conditions or those subject to recurrent respiratory infection and hemophiliacs. Some years ago it was popular to place these children in a separate classroom where they could be "protected." The present tendency is to attempt to provide proper safeguards while leaving them in a regular classroom. Lowered vitality cases deserve careful consideration but ideas relating to "what to do" with them are undergoing a definite change.

Homebound and/or Hospitalized Children

Homebound children may be physically handicapped or lowered vitality cases. More often, however, they are homebound or hospitalbound on a temporary basis due to accident or illness. These children need help in keeping up with classmates at school. This is usually accomplished through a teacher of the homebound or through a home-to-school two-way communication system. The special teacher may also go to the hospital to extend the services of the school, or the electrical equipment is sometimes used in the hospital setting. Some larger hospitals have their own teaching staff.

Emotionally Disturbed and/or Socially Maladjusted

The terms "emotionally disturbed" and "socially maladjusted" are properly descriptive of this group. There are problems relating to degree of disturbance and method of diagnosis, but these are overshadowed by questions regarding just what should be done with these children when they are identified. Certainly a great deal more research must be completed before we have the best answers to proper handling of the emotionally disturbed child in the public school.

THE PROFESSIONAL STAFF OF A COMPLETE SPECIAL EDUCATION PROGRAM

It may be argued that there is no such thing as a complete special education program. This argument holds much merit, but the following outline is meant to include a brief description of the variety of staff which might be found in a city the size of Cincinnati, St. Louis or Denver. If the broad scope of services required in one of these larger cities is fully understood, it will be of value in determining just what services are needed in smaller cities and communities. It may be safely assumed that most any school system will need some of these personnel, some on a full time and perhaps some on a part-time or itinerant basis.

The Classroom Teacher of Educable Mentally Retarded

This special educator is found in more school systems than any other type. Certainly if we mean full-time personnel attached to an individual school, this would be true.

Requirements applying to teachers of the educable mentally retarded vary throughout the United States, but in general, the following would apply:

1. Certification to teach in the regular classroom (in some states the certification must be for teaching at the same age level as the level of special class to be taught).

2. Certain special course requirements, relating to mental retardation. In some states this is absolutely required; in others it is required, but waived on an emergency basis; in a few states, no specialized training is required.

3. To remain certified, teachers employed after certain specified "cut-off" dates, but who do not meet the requirements in either of the two sections above, are required to work at a specific rate toward meeting such requirements.

The classroom teacher of the educable mentally retarded should be a teacher who is definitely interested in individual pupils, since this is a more individualized teaching program than the regular classroom. He should be a person who can feel satisfaction through achievement of relatively small gains, and who is not too heavily oriented in terms of pure academic learning. He should *not* have any overly strong, *emotionally oriented* motivation for teaching the mentally retarded.

Recent studies conducted by the Office of Education indicate that teachers presently in this field are somewhat critical of their own competency, and are strongly motivated toward a considerable amount of both in-service training and additional university training. It is obvious that in all but the largest school systems, teachers of the educable mentally retarded are much more "on their own" than regular classroom teachers. They must be alert to keep up with curriculum developments in a rapidly developing specialty area. Usually they belong to some local and/or national organizations relating to exceptional or retarded children. They are often called upon to give talks to community groups about their teaching assignment. They cannot be expected to be "super-teachers," but it certainly helps if they can approach the master teacher level of proficiency. Unlike some regular classroom teachers, there are few "lukewarm" teachers of the mentally retarded.

The Classroom Teacher of the Trainable Mentally Retarded

A teacher of this group does less academic teaching than any of the other various special education teachers. His work is with boys and girls who cannot be "educated" in the traditional sense of the word. For this reason, only about half of the communities in the United States who could have a trainable class, actually have such a class. Only a few of our teacher training institutions have a well-defined training program for this class level, and the large universities tend to be interested in the "psychology of the retarded" rather than the teaching or training methods. A teacher of the trainable groups must be able to set preschool level goals for boys and girls of junior high age—and be happy if half of them attain these goals. If the present direction of movement (both nationally and locally) is maintained, there will be many more trainable classes by 1970. The present movement away from institutionalization in state schools, and toward the local schools, community centers, and sheltered workshops, is here to stay. The teacher of the trainable, whose major goals may be self-sufficiency in dressing, toileting, and personal care, is becoming an essential member of the local special education team.

The Classroom Teacher of the Gifted

A person of this caliber is one to be highly regarded and much sought after. It is true that even a not-too-competent teacher can teach the gifted; they learn in spite of her. But a good teacher for the gifted is difficult to find for many of the same reasons as indicated in discussing the teacher of the mentally retarded. Good training centers for teachers of the gifted are few and far between, some are outstanding, but there are too many mediocre ones. This teacher needs to be well-informed in various subject areas, but must be even better informed as to the nature of learning. It is well for her to have access to a multitude of materials and specialized equipment, but it is much more important for her to understand and really appreciate how the gifted child differs from the normal one. She (the teacher) does not necessarily have to be "gifted" but she had better be more intelligent than average. She should understand why normal teaching methods are "too much" of "too little"—that is, too much time taken to learn small and insignificant concepts, and too little expected of children with much learning equipment. If, for example she is tied to conventional lockstep developmental reading, or drill methods in teaching arithmetic, she should stay away from the classroom for the gifted. If she can think in terms of big ideas and concepts, can work with seminar-type groups without losing pupil control, and if she understands that gifted children often "skip" many steps in traditional thinking patterns, she is on her way to success in teaching the gifted. Incidentally, this is a hard, tough grind, one which may require much more daily preparation than any other area of exceptionality.

The Classroom Teacher of the Deaf

She will be considered here as one who teaches a group of deaf and severely hard-of-hearing children in a self-contained classroom. (The resource room for the hard-of-hearing group will be considered later.)

The teacher of the deaf will probably be trained as a regular class teacher, and in addition, as a teacher of the deaf. Somewhere along the line she may have received training as a speech therapist. She will consider, as the major initial task, the teaching of language to these deaf children. It is true that for many years the deaf were taught by signs, but now even the incidental use of signs is fought in a never-ending war by the good teacher of the deaf. Her one overriding concern is language development on the part of her pupils. It may be said that she must be not only an excellent teacher in the ordinary sense of the word, but must also be highly trained in lip (speech) reading, and particularly in one of the specialized methods of teaching oral language to the deaf.

The Classroom Teacher of the Blind

A person trained for this class will more probably be found only in larger communities. Many times, parents who have a blind child will move to a large metropolitan area just to have public school classes available for their child. In areas where public school special classes are not available, blind children are generally sent to a state (boarding) school. A few blind children are simply integrated in regular classes, sometimes with amazing success. Teachers of the blind must have regular teacher training and certification, as well as training in special techniques for teaching the blind, including Braille. Many states also require a teacher of the blind to have experienced supervised teaching with the blind before certification. This area of teaching exceptional children is sufficiently specialized so that very few teachers "slip into" this type of teaching without adequate specialized training.

The Classroom Teacher of the Emotionally Disturbed (or Socially Maladjusted)

This person must be, first of all, well-adjusted and "even-tempered." She must be well-versed in teaching methods and goals for the normal classroom, but must understand also that these academic learning goals are secondary in her classroom. Children in a class for emotionally disturbed initially must become better adjusted and more stable before educational goals relating to reading and arithmetic can be realized. This teacher understands that just as a radio receiver will not receive a signal if it is not tuned in, so will a pupil not "receive a signal" if inner turmoil drowns out the message. This teacher must accept tremendous individual differences without being permissive to the point where bedlam reigns. She must understand how and when to set limits, and what limits to set. She must be well-trained in her specialty area and—though it is not a state requirement in most states—she should have "low blood pressure."

The Classroom Teacher of the Brain-Injured

Here is a specialist found only in larger population centers. There are some indications that the number of teachers required in this specialty area is increasing but one school of thought would tend to group the brain-injured with other exceptionalities. The teacher of the brain-injured must have competence as a regular classroom teacher, plus much specalized training in her specific area of exceptionality. She will require a special room arrangement and will have very specific furniture and equipment requirements. There are few universities or teachers' colleges training persons for this area of special education.

The Classroom Teacher of the Multiple Handicapped

This teacher is one who works with combinations of handicaps. Chicago, for example, employs teachers for at least nine different combinations of handicapping conditions. These are:

1. Physical and mental
2. Physical and deaf
3. Physical and blind
4. Physical and partially seeing
5. Physical and multiple
6. Physical and brain injury
7. Social and mental
8. Blind and mental
9. Deaf and mental

In a recent year in Chicago, nearly 700 pupils were listed as enrolled in classes for the multiple handicapped. It is obvious a teacher must have a combination of competencies to teach in one of these classes, the competencies varying in accordance with the combination of handicaps under consideration. It follows that certain highly specialized certification requirements can be established for these teaching positions, but the basic requirement for a teacher of the multiple handicapped is general teacher training, plus special training in areas of exceptionality involved in the handicapping areas served in the specific classroom. In many states there will be not a single classroom for the multiple handicapped.

The Classroom Teacher of the Orthopedically Handicapped

For this group a regular classroom teacher is required who has considerable special training in working with children with various orthopedic handicaps. She must know more about individualizing instruction than the regular classroom teacher because she may have several grade levels represented in her classroom. She must *not* be sympathetic, since children in her class do not need sympathy. She often works with the physical therapist and the occupational therapist, and must follow medical instructions. She must be able to tolerate many interruptions because boys and girls may leave her room at various times for work with the occupational, physical, or speech therapist.

The Resource Room Teacher of the Hard-of-Hearing

A person in this area is playing an increasingly important role in public school education of the hard-of-hearing child. There is a relatively large number of boys and girls who have sufficient hearing loss to cause serious problems when enrolled in a regular classroom, yet problems not serious enough to require an absolutely self-contained special class. These pupils usually make use of a hearing device, and with the recent development of transistorized, high-fidelity equipment, a new type of small, attractive, highly effective desk model units are available for classroom use. The resource room teacher meets regularly with boys and girls who use these desk units, and works with them on lip-reading techniques and general language development problems. Usually, she meets these children once each day; her work is highly correlated with that of the regular classroom where the child spends the remainder of the day. Therefore, the resource room teacher must work very closely with the regular classroom teacher—so this ability to work with other teachers is a prime requisite for the resource room teacher. The resource room teacher must be trained as a regular classroom teacher, with emphasis on language arts and reading skills, and must have additional training in speech pathology and methods of teaching the deaf. Often this teacher will have completed her undergraduate work in elementary education, plus considerable graduate work in the more specialized area of teaching the deaf.

The Resource Room Teacher of the Visually Handicapped

This teacher works in a manner similar to that described in the discussion relating to the hard-of-hearing. Because language skills are learned more through hearing than through seeing, the major problem for the partially sighted is magnification. Many of the bulky, hard-to-use magnifying devices have been more recently replaced by magnifiers produced primarily for factory use in inspection of machine tooling and similar industrial uses. These magnifiers have reduced the need for a large print books, making it possible for the visually handicapped to use the same text as other pupils, do map work at their desks and a variety of similar tasks. This has made it possible for many visually handicapped youngsters to remain in the regular classroom with a minimum of additional aid. When extra help is needed, these children are then enrolled in a school where the resource room is located; here they receive intensive help in groups of no more than three or four. Sometimes a resource room teacher may serve in a building in one section of town for half of each day, and in a building in another section of town for the other half-day. This teacher, like those in most of the other areas of handicap, must first be an effective teacher with a good general knowledge of teaching methods and classroom procedures. A reasonable amount of additional work in this special area will then qualify her to teach in the resource room for visually handicapped.

Speech Therapists

Members of this group are probably the second largest in number among special educators (teachers of the mentally retarded are the largest group) and serve more children than any other division of special educators. Simply stated, the purpose of the speech therapist is to help speech-handicapped school children develop more effective communication in interpersonal relationships. In many school systems, this type of help applies to the hearing handicapped in a similar manner, although growing specialization may bring about rapid changes in the very near future. Because a major portion of the educational program depends on reading, and reading progress is highly related to speech, this particular area of special education is quite important to relatively large numbers of individuals. Group work, using speech improvement techniques with a total classroom, has found considerable favor in some communities. This is usually done in kindergarten or first grade. The major work of the speech therapist is with elementary age children, concentrating on the primary grades. Teacher referral is the most common method of "finding" speech cases, but screening the speech of all children in a given grade is also commonly practiced. Many therapists feel that such screening should be done in the second or third grade, since by then it may be assumed that deviations of speech are likely to be of functional or organic nature, rather than of the maturational types. Problems of articulation and certain nonfluencies are among the most common problems served in the public school. Speech problems related to cerebral palsy, or cleft palate problems, are more difficult but can be handled in many school systems. Severe stuttering is an example of a type problem which should be served through a speech clinic in all except the very largest school systems, which may have what amounts to their own speech clinic.

Most states presently permit certification of speech therapists on a bachelor's degree level training, but by 1970 many states will be requiring a graduate degree for school speech work. In general, therapists usually plan to work with boys and girls twice per week, working in pupil groups of two to four. In actual practice, case loads range from 70 to 120, but for best results the case load should not exceed 50 to 60. The size of a group and the amount of time spent per session depends on the severity and type of problem, the age of the child and the speech therapist's total load.

In many schools the speech therapist also takes care of hearing testing and working with the hard-of-hearing child. In this type of organization, the therapist does individual testing after referral by the classroom teacher, and screens total classroom groups in some designated pattern (i.e., every other grade level). When a hearing loss is discovered, the therapist must contact the parents and strive for a medical referral. The therapist should also work with classroom teachers on preferential seating, plus other pupil needs; in some situations the therapist is responsible for obtaining desk model hearing aids or other such equipment. Speech (lip) reading may also be instituted by the therapist.

Hearing Clinicians

These specialists are rapidly gaining recognition in all parts of the United States as an essential part of the special education team. They are doing many tasks formerly undertaken by speech therapists, but are equipped to do a more thorough job because of their more specialized training, as well as the fact that they also are not charged with the year-round assignment of conducting a program of speech correction. The hearing clinician conducts group hearing screening and undertakes individual audiometric evaluations on a referral basis. He is free (timewise) to follow up on medical referrals to make certain the child does get to the physician. He serves as a consultant to classroom teachers regarding preferential seating of the hard-of-hearing child, probably doing a minimum of work of the same type as the teacher of the resource room for hard-of-hearing. He operates on an itinerant basis; his presence in the school system makes the work of the speech therapist more effective.

The Teacher of the Homebound and/or Hospitalized

Here is a service which has been a part of special education for many years. This teacher usually serves a small number of children who will never be able to attend regular school. Usually bedridden, they may go through all twelve years of public schooling without ever actually being present in a school. Another group, larger in number, are those recovering from a temporary illness or accident; for this group, homebound instruction is a way of "keeping up" until they can return to school.

The traditional homebound service consists of home instruction, three to five times per week, for periods of up to two hours. Obviously the teacher of the homebound cannot carry a very great pupil load when using this plan.

Sometimes the regular classroom teacher becomes a temporary teacher of the homebound, working an hour each day after school with a particular child. (If this is to continue more than a few days, additional remuneration is in order.)

Teaching by telephone is a method which is growing in popularity and is quite practical in junior and senior high school. Many school systems also use this system in grades four through six with considerable success. Telephone companies can install this two-way communication system at a nominal fee; if the teacher of the homebound is available to help initiate this system, it is a valuable supplement to the total home teaching program. Execu-tone, Inc., has a separate special education division dealing with the problems of teaching by telephone. A handbook entitled, *How to Teach Shut-In Students by Telephone* may be obtained from Executone; it will supply most of the needed answers relating to this exceptionally fine service to handicapped boys and girls.

It seems obvious that the one major requirement for the home teacher is that he be a jack-of-all-trades educationally; a well-trained educational generalist.

The Work-Study Coordinator

This specialist is a relatively new member of the special education team, working primarily in the area of mental retardation. In school programs where as many as three or four high-school level classes for educable mentally retarded exist, a work-study coordinator is most essential, at least on a half-time basis. When as many as seven or eight of these particular classes are involved, a full-time work-study coordinator is needed. It is the function of the coordinator to help prepare pupils, through individual or small-group counseling, to be ready for and capable of handling employment which is appropriate to their age.

This readiness is then "tested" through selected placement on a variety of jobs within the school and in the community. The work-study coordinator maintains close contact with the various employment stations, assisting the individual student to perform well in his employment. He also uses information gained regarding individual pupils to help all children in the program.

The work-study coordinator works very closely with the vocational rehabilitation counselor in gaining the benefits of all services of the division of vocational rehabilitation. In school systems which are apparently too small to justify a full-time work-study coordinator, this position may be successfully combined with that of the consultant in mental retardation.

The Occupational Therapist

A therapist in this field is more usually found in a separate special school setting; he works with the physically handicapped child in an attempt to help him overcome his disability. He has two main goals. The first relates to more adequate use of the physical self, and is called "functional therapy." Physicians will prescribe certain physical restoration goals for patients with weak muscles or stiff joints. The second procedure may be called "psychological therapy." Children may be very concerned about the ways in which they differ from other children; such therapy should help them over this hurdle.

States which recognize the occupational therapist as part of the public school special education team usually certify only occupational therapists graduated from a university which offers a training program approved by the American Medical Association. They must take a four-year undergraduate program plus a nine-month clinical internship. It is not easy to find a good occupational therapist who wants to do public school work; when one is found, he will usually require a higher salary than that provided by the regular teacher's salary schedule.

The Physical Therapist

This specialist is also more usually found in a separate special school setting. Whereas an occupational therapist may use games, hobbies, and similar interests as tools of his trade, the physical therapist will use exercise and various self-help devices such as braces, special chairs, and splints. Obviously the physical and occupational therapist work closely together, with both working under the direction of a medical doctor. There are two kinds of training programs for physical therapists: the first is a four-year undergraduate program planned specifically for this purpose; and the second requires approximately one and one-half years of graduate work beyond the bachelor's degree. Physical therapists, like occupational therapists, are in short supply.

The School Psychologist

The services of the school psychologist are rapidly gaining in prestige and importance throughout the United States. Better training programs are developing in our universities, and the American Psychological Association is taking more notice of their place in the hierarchy of this field. The typical training program is either a two-year master's degree or a Ph.D. program. The psychologist should have considerable knowledge of the workings of a public school to be of any great value to a school system. His major area of service is in diagnostic study of the individual child, but for his recommendations to make sense, he must understand practical limitations of the local school system. His diagnostic tools may include individual tests of intelligence or tests to determine type and severity of reading problems and causal factors. He must be able to assess and evaluate school records accurately and meaningfully, as well as gaining understanding of the child through classroom observation. He will serve as an advisor to the principal, the teacher and the parent.

In addition to testing, evaluation and interpretation of results to school staff and parents, the psychologist must be informed as to all available community agencies and be able to make referrals to them as necessary.

Psychologists may recommend children for special class placement or give an opinion regarding educability or emotional instability of a child, but they should *not* be asked to handle the administrative implementation of these recommendations.

In addition to all of these functions, there is an increasing trend toward using the school psychologist and his knowledge of learning theory for the general educational task of curriculum building. Perhaps, by definition, this is not a "special education function," but it is certainly an encouraging practice.

The School Social Worker

This person may be employed to serve public school children through case work practices, consultation with school personnel and counseling parents and children. Responsibilities and functions might be listed as follows:

1. Develop individual case reports of public school children who require special education services
2. Interpret the findings of such reports and make recommendations to the school personnel, to parents, and, when appropriate, to agencies and specialists
3. Assist school personnel and parents in developing understanding of the child as well as his situation, and assist in improving or alleviating the situation
4. Serve as a liaison between the school, community agencies and other resources to facilitate and coordinate services to children requiring special education
5. Obtain social histories of all children assigned to special education classes
6. Provide in-service education for teachers and school administrators
7. Develop public understanding and support of social work in public schools
8. Evaluate and report annually to the school administrator the nature and the extent of the present school social work services, and the indications of the present and future needs for such services.

Special Consultants or Coordinators

Such specialists may be needed for programs for the mentally retarded, for speech services, and for other areas of special education in larger school systems. When there are as many as twenty-five teachers of the mentally retarded, it is necessary that a consultant or supervisor be employed to work with them. The consultant's job would be training new teachers, building curriculum, and working with the teacher when there are especially difficult problems. This is particularly needed when these teachers are "spread out" in many schools throughout the school system.

A "head speech therapist" on a half-time basis (half-time with her own speech cases—half-time as a supervisor) is desirable when the speech therapy staff reaches eight to ten in number. School systems with fifteen or more speech therapists should have a full-time person, under the director of special education, but in charge of the speech therapy staff.

Various other consultants or supervisors may be needed in larger school systems, but these two are more likely to be needed first.

The Director of Special Education

A director is obviously the key person in the special education team. He must know enough about the various exceptionalities to develop a good program, and must recognize a quality program when he sees it. He must be able to find good personnel for his staff—or at least help the personnel director find them. He must have considerable administrative ability and be well enough informed about the general school program to be able to work efficiently with those in charge of other departments of the school system. In most school systems he will need to know a great deal about parent counseling, but at the same time will need to be well-informed regarding local school budget, state budgeting procedures and problems, and the state reimbursement plan.

Until very recent years, not many of our training institutions recognized the dual role (administrator-special education expert) required of the director of special education, but more recently some good training programs have developed at the doctoral level. Finding a good director of special education is not too different from finding a good director of curriculum, of elementary education, or of any other major division of the public school. If job descriptions are carefully written, and an attractive salary is offered, competent people are available for the job.

III

Financing the Special Education Program

GENERAL DISCUSSION

IT is not practical to discuss the problems involved in financing the special education program without first taking a look at the problems involved in financing the total educational program. There are three general types of support for public education. First, there is pure local support. Second, there is state support (this might take any of a dozen or more forms). Third, there is Federal Government support. Despite the fact that state responsibility for the educational program within it has been commonly accepted for some years, local help must still bear the major load of financing the public school system in most of our country today. The state support theory and some of the discussion which is generally given favoring such support will be reviewed here because of the direct bearing it has on support of special education.

In reviewing state aid, the function of this support must be established. Three basic theories regarding this function might be summarized as follows:

The partial equalization theory is based on the accepted fact that each district's financial ability to support public education is quite different from every other district's ability. The number of children per 1,000 population in various school districts varies greatly, and the arbitrary method in which school district boundaries are established in many parts of our country may give rise to extreme financial hardship. Under a partial equalization plan, money is distributed in amounts needed to bring the "poorer" districts up to some minimum state standard. With this plan, all districts levy some local taxes, but poorer districts may receive a great deal of state support, while more wealthy districts receive very little state financial aid.

The stimulation theory is advocated by those who see the function of the state as that of a stimulator of certain selected programs which might not appear to the public as essential, but in the opinion of educational experts, are imperative if we are to provide equal opportunity for all children. Under this plan, wealthy or poor school districts may receive equal amounts of state funds if they put into effect the programs which these funds were designed to initiate or promote. Indications are that this is a very effective program. Representatives of local school districts report they are able to obtain approval for new programs because, due to state support, these new programs cost no more than the "regular" kind. Under this plan, the state may pay all of the cost of these particular programs, but generally will pay only the so-called "excess" cost.

The state support of the basic program theory is one which is being accepted by an increasing number of lay persons. They are beginning to feel that anything short of this type support is quite unfair to many taxpayers. For example, one man may live across the street (and across a school district line) from another man with property of equal sale value, yet may pay a school tax bill many times higher than that which his neighbor pays. And the child of the man who pays the lesser tax bill may have the better school situation. This results from such factors as where the county line happens to be, the ratio of school-age children to adults in the area, the location of one or several large plants or factories. Such factors as who knows whom, and, therefore, where the new defense plant is built may give rise to a series of serious inequities in a particular area. More and more people, including many outside the field of education, have come to the conclusion that despite problems such as raising the money, distributing it fairly and equitably, and supervising and assuring the maintenance of a minimum or basic quality program (that is, assuring that the money is properly used), the theory of total state support of a basic educational program is the most workable and desirable.

Federal support, though much discussed (and much misunderstood) has been a theory accepted in practice in certain special areas for many decades. Federal support of the school lunch program, the vocational education program, the program to stimulate a more effective system of guidance and counseling, the program to promote the development of more adequate and complete laboratories in the science area, and many others are well accepted. One of the larger federally-supported educational enterprises in the past was the so-called G.I. Bill and its educational provisions. Another type of help is represented by the various graduate fellowship programs and research projects in our public schools, colleges and universities which are carried out entirely on the basis of Government support. Federal aid to areas where school enrollments are increasing out of all reasonable proportion due to the proximity of defense plants, air bases and missile sites has been the only means whereby some of these areas have been able to "keep their heads above water."

Federal aid is easily defensible if we believe that all children in America should have equal opportunities to develop themselves to the full extent of their ability. On a more personal basis, if we want our neighbors and fellow citizens in our community to be enlightened and well-informed, if we recognize the fact that some states have low quality school programs and that children who are the product of these programs are quite likely to move to another state, we are forced to consider some scheme which will bring all school systems, in every community of every state, up to some sort of basic minimal standard of excellence. Perhaps some day we will see a program of Federal aid which will bring about his condition.

Obviously, if local support cannot in many areas support a good program of general education, it will be even more difficult to find the money for a program with a much more expensive per-pupil-cost. With this in mind, it is easy to see why most of the states which support special education use some form of the "stimulation" method. Generally, these states pay the excess teacher costs (i.e., if the teacher is limited to fifteen special education pupils rather than a normal load of thirty, the state pays half of her salary). The state may also pay all of the costs of certain special equipment needed, and may pay up to 70 or 80 per cent of the salary of the director of special education or supervisors of the special education program. Where county personnel are needed to serve two or three counties or where many small districts are joined together in a cooperative program in more sparsely populated areas, the state usually pays approximately half of the salary and may also pay a rather liberal transportation allowance.

These examples of application of the "stimulation" method are over-simplifications, but, along with the summaries of state financial support which follow, should accurately represent the type of state financial aid provided for various special education programs. The following summaries were gathered from state regulations relating to special education reimbursement; they were selected by the writer as representative of two main possibilities.

State A: Special Education Reimbursement

Special education personnel who are not classified as classroom teachers are eligible for reimbursement on an 80 per cent of "cost" basis. This reimbursement applies to salary and travel expenses incurred by the local district during the school year where such payments are made directly to the special education personnel involved. This category would include directors; supervisors; consultants; psychologists; speech therapists; audiologists; itinerant or resource room teachers of the blind, deaf, emotionally disturbed, and teachers of the homebound.

Special education classroom teachers such as teachers of the retarded; the physically handicapped; emotionally disturbed; deaf; or hard-of-hearing, and blind or partially sighted (where these are self-contained classes) and others as approved under existing regulations, will be reimbursed on an excess cost basis in amounts not to exceed those established by certain formulas. (The formulas then provide for reimbursement in amounts which will not generally exceed 50 per cent of the teacher's salary.) The reasoning here is that children have to be in a classroom somewhere, and the only excess cost of the special education class is due to small class size, usually mandatory to meet state standards.

Maximum group size is a part of this formula, which is related to age range within the class; the plan rewards smaller age ranges and class sizes from twelve to fifteen pupils.*

Certain equipment and materials may be borrowed from the state office of special education or may be purchased by local districts and then "sold" to the state at the end of the year. These items (100 per cent reimbursed) include such things as magnifying devices for visually handicapped; brailled material for the blind; hearing devices for the hard-of-hearing; special adaptive devices for the physically handicapped (if they are re-usable) and other similar items. After this total reimbursement they become the property of the state, but may be requisitioned for the next school year.

Special transportation costs, up to a limit of three hundred dollars per pupil, per year, are reimbursed on what amounts to about a 50 per cent basis.

Various special services such as reader service for the blind, electrical home-to-school service for the homebound and others may be reimbursed up to 50 per cent of cost.

"Pilot programs" of an innovative or demonstration nature, if approved in advance by the state director of special education, will be reimbursed on a total cost basis.

State B: Special Education Reimbursement

The state will reimburse for all properly endorsed and fully approved special education personnel on the following basis:

Director of Special Education	$6,000
Supervisor of Consultant in Special Education	5,000
School Psychologist	4,500
All other professional personnel	3,000

---

* In the first two categories under "State A" the teachers or other personnel must be approved by the state department of special education; classes and/or services must meet certain state established standards to be eligible for reimbursement. State reports must be submitted as per established regulations, state meetings must be attended. If a school district attempts to place an ineligible pupil in a class and is apprehended, it will lose reimbursement in connection with that class. Also note that this state has not paid more than two-thirds of the reimbursement "promised" by these standards in recent history.

Reimbursement for special equipment and/or materials for various handicapping conditions will be made on a 50 per cent of cost basis, not to exceed two dundred dollars cost per pupil program ($200 = 50 per cent of $400 total cost). This will include such items as special hearing devices, brailled material (total cost for year limit—four hundred dollars approvable, resulting in two hundred dollars reimbursement). Equipment and material purchases must be approved by the state director of special education *in advance*. Most consumable materials will *not* be approved.

We should note that it is an unfortunately common practice for a state legislature to pass laws which would lead one to expect a certain percentage of reimbursement, and then provide funds for only half, or even less than half of the amount indicated in the basic legislation. Therefore, a comparison of what state reimbursement laws indicate is not always too meaningful if the primary concern is actual financial support of special education. The most meaningful comparisons which may be made relate to how much each state *actually pays* local districts for various programs.

The Elementary and Secondary Education Act of 1965

The Elementary and Secondary Education Act (ESEA) of 1965, particularly Title I, had sweeping ramifications for special education. In a number of local school districts across the country, implementation of this act was simply "turned over" to directors of special education.

Officials of the Office of Education held a number of regional meetings in late fall and early winter of 1965, "inviting" directors of special education, who could also bring their superintendents. ESEA brought considerable money to local districts, thus many school districts were able to upgrade and expand their special education programs by as much as 20 to 30 per cent.

The ESEA, along with the various amplifying and explanatory bulletins, would fill several volumes, but in essence it may be summarized as follows: (This applies for the most part to Title I, which involved the most money, and was directly applicable to special education.)

1. This legislation was designed to stimulate the provision of better school opportunities for educationally deprived children.
2. Money was allocated in a manner which led to specific sums being available to local school districts which developed acceptable plans for its use.
3. The program was channeled through state departments of education.
4. The amount of money available was directly proportional to the number of low income families in the public school district.
5. The ESEA proposal had to be coordinated with any local programs of the Office of Economic Opportunity (War on Poverty).
6. Benefits of ESEA programs were required to be made available to pupils in private schools.
7. (Last and probably most important.) Monies allotted under Title I of ESEA were paid to school districts *before* they actually made the expenditures indicated on their project applications.

The bill was passed early in 1965 but funds to put the bill into operation were not authorized until just after schools opened in the fall. School districts (with already approved budgets, and property tax requests previously set) could not employ new personnel until it was certain that money was available. As any school personnel director knows, you do not look for and just "find" a dozen or so highly specialized school personnel (for example, school psychologists, speech therapists, teachers of the blind) in September or October. This led to many districts having to hire personnel who were somewhat less qualified than would seem desirable for the highly specialized positions involved.

The question of how to provide services for private school children raised the issue of separation of school and state. The funds went to the public schools, but private school pupils were also to be helped. Questions were asked such as: Should private school children be scheduled for speech therapy in the public school? or Should the speech therapist (employed through ESEA funds) go to the private school? Power politics and resultant political pressure from both the public and the private school points of view came to bear on boards of education, superintendents, and directors of special education.

ESEA funds were all tied to the prerequisite of compliance with laws relating to nondiscrimination. This subject requires no explanation to make clear the various crosscurrents and whirlpools of emotion, and political pressures unleashed.

At any rate, ESEA ushered in a new era of financing by the Federal Government using a "payment-in-advance" rather than "payment-after-you've-spent-it" philosophy.

It should be mentioned that other sections of the ESEA also benefited special education on the local level, but in less direct ways. Under one title, studies might be made to determine the feasibility of intermediate or cooperative districts for provision of better services to children. Under another title, state departments of education could be strengthened. Almost every state took advantage of this title so that state level special education staffs were greatly improved. Other related provisions also resulted in improvements for special education, but the major help came through addition of staff, equipment, and materials through Title I.

More recent legislation, implemented in 1967, placed ESEA special education monies under a new section, Title VI. This new title, if funded as proposed, will be highly significant in the future development of special education.

Financing in the Cooperative, Intermediate, or Separate Special Education Districts

One of the more promising practices for financing and properly developing programs of special education relates to the organization of cooperative, intermediate, or special school districts. This, of course, requires legislative provision, but the past several years have been good ones in this respect. A general discussion of this type organization may be found in the chapter on cooperative and overlying districts, but three examples will be cited here and discussed with relation to financial advantages.

Suburban Chicago has had cooperative special education programs for a number of years. These may serve as many as 20 to 25 smaller districts, and for the most part are the vehicle whereby expert administrative and supervisory staff are provided. Classroom teachers for various specialized areas of exceptionality are ordinarily employed by the local districts, with smaller districts sending children on a tuition basis to established classes. Through joint or cooperative effort, such personnel as a director, psychologists, supervisors for various classes, and clerical staff for this operation are employed. The various districts contribute on a basis related to pupil enrollment; relatively good financial reimbursement is received from the state, both for special education employees who work directly for the local district, and for those engaged in the cooperative district effort. This is a highly satisfactory arrangement, quite workable in most suburban areas.

In Wisconsin, a somewhat different approach is taken. Through state legislation, nineteen cooperative educational service agencies have been established which cover the entire state. These districts are to conduct such programs as research, special classes, data collection and library or audio-visual services. The agency can provide only those services desired by local districts, and therefore does not in any way dictate to the local district. This cooperative service agency replaced the county superintendent system, which represented a real advance in provision of educational services to smaller school districts. Though these service agencies were not specifically established to foster special education, the end result is that more services to handicapped pupils are made available. Unlike the Illinois plan (where the director of the Cooperative Special Education program is paid by contributions from various districts) in Wisconsin the agency administrator is paid from state funds. Also, secretarial, office and travel costs are paid from state funds. In both states the various districts contribute to the employment of such personnel as speech therapists, psychologists and others.

In St. Louis County (Missouri) a considerably different plan is in operation. From the point of view of the special education administrator, this scheme is probably the most ideal. Here, by special legislative provision, an overlying district was given separate taxing authority to provide services for handicapped children. This district has its own board of directors elected from subdivisions of the district, and its own complete administrative structure for the sole purpose of providing educational programming for handicapped boys and girls.* In the St. Louis plan, the special education district leases rooms from local districts, and in some cases "purchases" transportation services (whenever this proves to be less expensive than using its own buses). The two outstanding advantages of this plan are:

First, the board of directors has as its major concern the provision of quality education for handicapped boys and girls. (In the typical school system, where handicapped children represent a small per cent of the total school population, the board obviously has much less time for special education.)

Second, the special education board has control (under statutory limits) of taxing authority. The disadvantage of the St. Louis plan is that, at present, such separate, additional taxing-body type plans are almost impossible to pass through the typical state legislative hurdles.

In any of these plans, or others discussed in the chapter on cooperative or overlying districts, the financial advantage relates to one or a combination of the following factors:

1. Broader tax base
2. Larger district, thus providing far more economical grouping of pupils
3. School board which has special education as a primary responsibility
4. More favorable reimbursement from state sources.

In any event, the cooperative district is evolving rapidly and has great significance in the financing of programs of special education.

In any discussion of existing state (or Federal) financing of educational programs, the question of how to get where we think

---

* More recently the St. Louis County plan was expanded to include a vocational-technical school program.

we want to go should not be overlooked. On the state level it is well to find out which state legislators are most interested in education, then work on these individuals. Of particular importance are members of the education committee and members of the budget committee. Obviously, the state superintendent of schools (or state commissioner) must be influenced; he should be involved in special education planning, if at all possible. Because of the tremendous importance of legislation, all educators must play a role in shaping the future of laws relating to education.

IV

Cooperative Special Education Districts

IF there is any real hope of extending special education services to smaller school districts, it is through the development of some type of cooperative inter-district plan. If there are to be services for medium-sized school districts beyond the more traditional special education programs which serve the more frequently-observed handicapping conditions, they will be provided through some sort of joint programming with adjoining districts. Even where a number of adjacent districts have provided (for example) adequate programs for the educable mentally retarded, individual district size may prohibit (in terms of economic efficiency) the employment of a curriculum coordinator to help improve the program, or a work-study coordinator to assist in the vital function of school-to-work articulation. However, if a number of districts band together, these positions become relatively easy to justify and to support financially.

Joint programs are now a fact in many states, thus the following examples are somewhat representative of the total gamut of such cooperative program planning. The author has deliberately chosen five Mid-western states—Illinois, Wisconsin, Iowa, Missouri, and Michigan—to prove that this area of the nation (which some educators in other sections would characterize as "traditional" or "conservative") does make provision for relatively exemplary plans for cooperative services. If the conservative Midwest can do this, the rest of the nation certainly can.

Cooperative Planning: The Illinois "Joint Agreement" Plan

An absolute prerequisite to any type of joint school district planning is the legislation making such planning possible. A sample of such legislation may be found in the following sections of the School Code of the State of Illinois:

> Section 19-22.31. Special Education. To enter into joint agreements with other school boards to establish programs for children of the type described in Section 14-1, to provide the needed special educational facilities, and to employ a director and other professional workers for such programs. The director may be employed by one district and such district shall be reimbursed by other districts that are parties to the agreement on a mutually agreed basis. Such agreements may provide that one district may supply professional workers for a joint program conducted in another district.

In Illinois there is a statutory requirement that the county superintendent call together the school boards of districts which are not meeting special educational needs, and at this mandatory planning conference, recommend a plan to meet such needs. It is not *required* by law that boards of education follow such recommendations, but the implication is there, and provision for cooperative interdistrict planning is available and workable.

A joint agreement in Illinois is a formal plan, clearly stating the conditions of joint operation for this specific program. The agreement is valid only after each school board in the proposed cooperative area has acted favorably on the proposed joint agreement. Representatives of the Division for Exceptional Children of the Office of Public Instruction are available to consult with local districts in establishing such a program, but in practice, the following sub-areas are usually included in any agreement:

1. Scope of the proposal and philosophical rationale
2. Legal names of districts involved
3. Provision for expanding or amending agreement
4. Specific terms of the agreement as of the date of initiation (these to be spelled out in an addendum and the actual agreement to be signed by cooperating districts will simply refer to such an addendum)

The terms of the agreement which may be covered in an addendum will possibly include the following:

1. A clear-cut statement as to the method of making decisions for the total cooperative program

2. A procedure for selecting a director for the program
3. The location of the administrative office
4. The location of the initial special classes
5. Method of selecting professional staff
6. Salaries, supervision, and provision for salary increases
7. Method of determining tuition costs
8. Co-responsibilities of, as well as between the various districts in the larger cooperative district, and the relationship of the director to these districts
9. Methods of handling applications, claims, records, reports, transportation problems and other such administrative detail

The usual procedure in Illinois is to designate one of the participating districts as the one with primary administrative responsibility (usually the one which can house the director and the administrative offices). Other districts are then called "member" districts. A plan is provided to determine what the financial share of each member district should be (based on a formula in the school code) and tuition is charged each participating district, after adjusting for reimbursement received by the administrative district.

If the best proof of a plan is in terms of obtained results, the Illinois plan must be rated as successful. Much of the credit for its success should go to special educators and general educators in the state who supported the legislation which makes the plan workable. This plan has developed over a number of years and may well be considered as one of several different types of successful, cooperative district plans.

Cooperative Planning: The Wisconsin Plan

The Wisconsin concept of the Cooperative Educational Service Agency is a relative newcomer to the cooperative district scene. Because of its comparative newness, and because it was developed to help provide various educational services (not just special education), it represents an interesting model for further study. Leaders in public education in Wisconsin have indicated there are two dates in Wisconsin history which have outstanding significance with relation to the development of public education. The first date, 1863, marks the initiation of the county superintendency. The second, 1965, signaled the initiation of the Cooperative Educational Service Agency and the termination of the County Superintendency. It must be noted that county superintendents were part of the group which recommended the changes which led to formulation of the Cooperative Educational Service Agency. Section 39.51 of Chapter 565, Wisconsin Laws of 1963, describes the purpose of the educational service agency program. That section reads as follows:

> The organization of school districts in Wisconsin is such that there is a recognized need for some type of service unit between the local district and the state superintendent level. There is hereby created such units designed to serve educational needs in all areas of Wisconsin. Such cooperative educational service agencies are created by the state as a convenience for local districts in cooperatively providing special educational services to teachers, students, school boards, administrators, and others, and may include, but is not restricted because of enumeration, such programs as research, special student classes, data collection, processing and dissemination, in-service programs, and liaison between the state and local school districts.

This same legislation provided for a representative state-wide committee of eighteen persons to further develop plans to implement this law. The duties of this committee were carefully outlined and in fulfilling these duties, the committee made a number of recommendations.

Written into the original law were three criteria: First, there are to be no more than twenty-five agencies; second, no agency is to cross high school district boundaries and third, territory of an agency area is to be contiguous and compact as possible.

After its deliberations, the committee agreed to other criteria to be used as guidelines. They first agreed to strive for a maximum radius of sixty miles for any one district. They further agreed to attempt to establish a minimum of twenty-five thousand pupils enrolled in any one district.

In September, 1964, the committee adopted a tentative plan calling for nineteen districts (area agencies). A series of meetings to hear comments of the public were scheduled. After hearing and recording comments from hundreds of citizens, a number of revisions in district composition of the nineteen areas were made, and a final plan was adopted on November 24, 1964. Certain recommendations were made to the legislature which were incorporated in an amendment to the original legislation. Provisions for revision of agency boundaries by transfer of districts or consolidation of agencies were important features of this amendment.

As an end-result, by July 1, 1965, there were nineteen cooperative Educational Service Agencies, including all of the state of Wisconsin. These agencies ranged in pupil population from 18,300 to 193,800. In terms of number of local school districts included in each cooperative Educational Service Agency, districts varied from fourteen to sixty-three. Only one agency area included more than seventy-five thousand pupils, and only one included less than twenty thousand pupils. The following sections are taken from the law establishing the Cooperative Educational Service Agencies. Their importance in the understanding of the operation of these agencies is obvious.

Method of Selection of the Board of Control

39.55 COOPERATIVE EDUCATIONAL SERVICE AGENCY, GOVERNING BODY. (1) Each cooperative educational service agency created by the state cooperative service committee shall be governed by a board of control composed of one delegate from each school district board in the agency designated annually in July by such school board, but not more than eleven members. There shall be no more than one member on the board of control from the territory comprising each union high school district and the underlying school districts operating elementary grades only. For the purpose of determining representation on the board of control, a common school district operating elementary grades only, lying in more than one union high school district, shall be considered part of the union high school district in which the major proportion of its equalized valuation lies. Vacancies shall be filled as are original appointments. The first meeting of such board shall be called by the delegate from the school district in the service agency with the largest full valuation who shall act as temporary chairman. Such meeting shall be held on the 3rd Monday in March, 1965. The board of control shall hold an annual organizational meeting on the 2nd Monday in August.

(2) If there are more than eleven school districts in the service agency, the state superintendent shall cause to convene annually a convention composed of one delegate from each school district board in the agency. Upon the convening of the convention, the representatives from all boards of each union high school area, meeting separately, shall determine the delegate of the union high school to be announced prior to the selection of the board of control. For the purpose of determining the delegate of the union high school area, a representative from an elementary school district board shall be considered part of the union high school area in which the major proportion of its equalized valuation lies. After the meeting for the determination of delegates, the convention shall formulate a plan of representation for such service agency including no more than eleven delegates, which plan shall be effective at once.

SECTION 40. The provisions of this act relating to the state cooperative educational committee shall take effect upon passage and publication. All other provisions shall take effect July 1, 1965, except that section 39.55 of the statutes created by this act shall take effect March 1, 1965.

Functions of Board of Control

39.56 The cooperative educational service agency board of control shall:

(1) Determine the policies of the service agency.

(2) Receive state aids for operation of the cooperative service agency.

(3) Approve service contracts with local school districts, county boards of supervisors and other cooperative educational service agencies, but no such contracts shall extend beyond three years.

(4) Determine participating local unit's prorated share of the cost of cooperative programs and assess such costs against each participating unit, but no board of control may levy any taxes. No cost shall be assessed against a unit for a cooperative program unless the school district enters into a contract for such service.

(5) Appoint and contract with an agency coordinator, for a term of not more than three years, with qualifications established by rule of the state superintendent of public instruction, but at least equal to the highest level of certification required for local school district administrators, who shall be considered a teacher as defined by §42.20(13) and subject to ch. 42.

(6) Meet monthly and at the call of the chairman.

(7) Select a chairman, vice chairman, and treasurer from its membership at the annual organizational meeting. The coordinator shall act as a nonvoting secretary to the board of control. Vacancies shall be filled as are original appointments.

(8) Adopt bylaws for the conduct of its meetings.

(9) The board shall require a bond of the treasurer and the coordinator.

(10) Authorize the expenditure of money for the purposes set forth in this subchapter and for the actual and necessary expenses of the board and coordinator and for the acquisition of equipment, space, and personnel. All accounts of the agency shall be paid on voucher signed by the chairman and secretary.

(11) The board shall establish the salaries of the coordinator and other professional and nonprofessional employees. The salary of the coordinator shall be within the range of $10,500 to $13,500.

(12) Do all other things necessary to carry out the provisions of this subchapter.

The following description of the duties of the coordinator of the Cooperative Educational Service Agency is taken from the *Administrative Handbook,* Wisconsin Department of Public Instruction, Angus B. Rothwell, State Superintendent.

Duties of the Coordinator

The title of the person responsible for the administration of each cooperative educational service agency is Agency Coordinator. His duties are defined in §39.57 of Wisconsin Laws of 1963 as follows:

The agency coordinator shall be responsible for coordinating the services, securing the participation of the individual districts, county boards, and other cooperative educational service agencies and implementing the policies of the board of control.

The statute refers to the qualifications of the coordinator in these words, ". . . qualifications established by rule of the state superintendent of public instruction but at least equal to the highest level of certification required for local school district administrators. . . ." (§39.56(5)) The state superintendent has indicated that the inference in the wording above needs no further interpretation than that candidates for the coordinator's position must be eligible to hold a superintendent's license.

Boards of control are charged with the responsibility of appointing and contracting with an agency coordinator for a term of not more than three years. In its procurement efforts a board of control may find that it will receive applications. However, it may need to make efforts, as a board, to approach established sources of information concerning desirable candidates for the position, much as it would in hiring a school district administrator. The Teacher Placement Service of the Wisconsin State Employment Service in Madison; the Teacher

Placement Bureau of the University of Wisconsin in Madison and Milwaukee; the placement office of the Wisconsin State Universities; the placement office of other degree-granting institutions at the graduate level, within or out of the state, are in a position to be helpful in a search for qualified candidates. Most of the offices referred to will supply to authorized persons confidential, evaluative information concerning individuals qualified for the position of coordinator. Some boards may wish to make an analysis of the qualifications of a professional and personal nature that a coordinator ought to bring to his position. Certainly a knowledge of the substance of a good school program as gained from experience in teaching, school administration and personal professional study is important. An awareness of the fiscal and curricular problems and practices typical of today's schools is essential.

This person ought to possess the ability to visualize educational possibilities and gain support for proposed action by convincing presentations to school officials. Certainly he should be able to make recommendations by the "book," but ability to evaluate, to discard, and to create are qualities that will give his recommendations greater validity.

He ought to have strong faith in the whole institution of public education, but with a challenging attitude towards anything within it that fails to meet the test of critical scrutiny. As is true of anyone in a position of influence in the affairs of schools, his personal sensitivity to the meaningful things in life needs to be genuine or his leadership will lack pertinence and relevance. Like any leader, he needs that quality of commonness about him that makes for a comfortable relationship with people.

An analysis of the activities of the agency coordinator as prescribed by the law and as interpreted in the nature of the position produces several items.

1. He shall meet with the board of control monthly or more often as necessary.

2. He shall act as secretary to the board of control.

3. He ought to prepare agenda for meetings of the board of control as provided by the policies of the board.

4. He shall implement the policies of the service agency in promoting participation of school districts by maintaining close communication with school administrators and school boards.

5. He shall possess knowledge of modern school programs and the needs of schools of various types and sizes and present this information to school personnel as need, opportunity, and good judgment recommend.

6. He shall be prepared to call meetings of the advisory committee to obtain their counsel for himself and the board of control.

7. He shall maintain an office with the necessary facilities for communication with school districts and the personnel-providing cooperative services.

8. He shall interview and recommend to the board of control the candidates who are to provide services for the schools of the agency.

9. With the board of control he should develop a system of determining services desired by individual districts and executing contracts for these services between the agency and the school district.

10. He shall maintain records for determining pro rata share of school districts for services rendered.

11. He shall be bonded as directed by the board of control.

12. With the chairman of the board of control he shall audit the bona fide expenditures of the agency and sign authorized vouchers.

13. He shall maintain records such that state aids may be legally claimed, received, and properly accounted.

14. He shall attend meetings called by the State Superintendent under §39.02(18).

15. He shall act as secretary to the county school committees of the counties having the largest proportion of their equalized valuation in the agency which employs him.

16. He shall provide for gathering statistical information from agency districts and disseminating information to promote ". . . liaison between the state and local districts."

17. He shall carry on those activities which will provide for a business and professional like operation of the agency in keeping with the purpose of Chapter 565 as provided in Section 39.51.

A most careful scrutiny of the implementation of the Cooperative Educational Service Agency in Wisconsin will convince most observers that the plan was well conceived and carefully carried through. It is not a plan for special education alone, but certainly will greatly affect the development of special education programs. It has a distinct advantage over many cooperative plans in that it provides for the entire state to be included, and provides the salary for an administrator, plus office expenses. However, the concept of the autonomous school district was given an assist in that *first,* the supervisory, inspectatorial county superintendency was eliminated, and *second,* the new system relates to any local district *only* on a "request by the local district" basis. Also, the separate taxing authority of the county unit was eliminated and no new taxing system was instituted.

If local districts want a service from the Department of School Psychological Services, for example, they ask the agency administrator to try to arrange such service, and then they pay for the service they receive. Obviously, the administrator tries to arrange the need for services or personnel so that the districts may cooperatively "buy" services they could not easily arrange to obtain on an individual basis.

The St. Louis County Special District

The St. Louis (Missouri) County Special District is unique in Missouri and in the nation. In 1957, by vote of the people of St. Louis County, a new school district was created. This district covers the entire county, with responsibility only for those children who are defined as "handicapped" in Missouri School Law and in the regulations of the State Department of Education. The Board of Education of the Special District is elected from those who properly declare their candidacy from six approximately equal (population) areas of St. Louis County. Each year, two board members are elected; the operation of the board is similar to that of any board of education. At present, this district has an assessed valuation of approximately two billion dollars; the board may establish a tax levy of up to fifteen cents per one hundred dollars of assessed valuation. Assessment of additional funds can be approved by a majority vote of the citizens of that County. Total funds, including tax receipts and state funds for a recent year were nearly four million dollars.

As might be guessed from the amount of funds available to this single district, an exceptional program for handicapped children is carried on. A total of approximately four hundred professional personnel are employed, in addition to more than thirty administrative and supervisory personnel. Obviously, quantity does not necessarily mean quality, but because of the number of experts and the financial resources available, an excellent program can be implemented. No one of the twenty-five local districts included in this Special District could provide the variety of programs which are provided by the overlying Special District.

Among the many advantages of this program made possible

by the large population involved and the resultant financial support, are the following:

The Special District Evaluation Clinic. This clinic is used in case the original screening indicates need for further clinical evaluation, and includes the service of a pediatric consultant, an orthopedic consultant, and just about any type of expert and specialized consultant or diagnostician one might hope for in a truly ideal evaluation clinic.

A Research Program. The specific research emphasis varies from year to year, but the intent is to work with areas of specific concern to the Special District.

Inservice Training for Staff. Here again, staff size creates a real range of need, and helps make the provision of nationally and internationally famous lecturers and consultants a practical matter.

Actually, the St. Louis County Special District is not too different in size and scope from the special programs in several of our largest cities. However, without the legislative provision for the cooperative program to serve this area, there would likely be twenty-five districts, with twenty-five special education programs, and a number of less frequently encountered exceptionalities would simply not be served. Also, the Evaluation Clinic, and the "richness" of the inservice program would be impossible for any one, or even any two or three districts in combination.

Special District officials document an increase of inservice to pupils from less than 25 per cent of known handicapped children receiving service in 1957 when the District was established, to nearly 95 per cent receiving service five years later. This certainly seems to be adequate justification for this particular Special District.

Recently, the scope of this Special District was expanded to include responsibility for a post-high school vocational-technical training program. The tax levy limit of the Special District was increased appropriately, and the special education function was not adversely affected.

Cooperative Planning in Iowa: Two Different Plans

At least two different cooperative plans are now in operation in Iowa. One plan, which has been strongly encouraged by the Special Education Division of the State Department of Public Instruction, is called the *Multi-County Plan*. In Iowa, the major school taxes are levied by local districts, but a smaller amount is levied by the county superintendent of schools for various county-wide purposes. One of the major uses of this county school tax is for special education programming. State law provides for counties to operate a joint special education program, if they elect to do so. In the sparsely populated areas a number of three- and four-county units have been organized, and operate quite effectively. A usual plan is for the county superintendents and school boards who wish to form such a cooperative program to meet with state officials to establish the ground rules. Generally, a joint board is established which determines policy for the program, and which turns much of the responsibility for operational procedures over to the county superintendents of the counties involved. Since county superintendents in Iowa are appointed by the elected board members, this is a relatively safe procedure. This joint board and the county superintendents decide on the programs desired (again with the help of state consultants) employing a director and various other personnel as needed. Usually classroom teachers are employed by local districts, but the various districts then "trade" pupils, via the tuition route. The multi-county director plans the level of instruction required, makes actual pupil placement, and recommends need and location for additional classes and personnel. Speech therapists and school psychologists are usually employed by the cooperative unit and assigned in a manner determined by the joint board, the county superintendents and the director. Cost of the multi-county program is pro-rated to the various counties on the basis of average daily attendance for the counties involved. This plan has done a remarkable job of increasing and upgrading special education services in rural areas of Iowa.

A second plan is in use in various counties where there is a major school district comprising one-half or more of the population of the county. This is similar, in many respects, to the multi-county plan except that only one county is involved. Here the county board of education and county superintendent in effect "contract" with the major district to administer and supervise a program for the entire county. County school taxes are used to pay the cost of employing all itinerant personnel and any special education consultative personnel. Also, teachers for trainable retarded classes may be directly employed by the county superintendent and then serve the entire county, ignoring local district boundaries.

This plan may be accomplished by the county board employing these personnel, or by the county board paying the local board of the major school district to carry out the program. In either case, a definite agreement spelling out the manner in which these persons will operate, is essential. Also the manner of handling state reimbursement must be specifically delineated.

This plan has proved to be workable and advantageous in providing services for handicapped boys and girls.

Michigan's Intermediate District

Michigan is an example of a state which makes provision for the levying of an extra millage to be used exclusively for special education programming. In Michigan an intermediate school district is a county or multi-county district; the board of the intermediate district may make provisions for special education needs in a variety of ways. If a local school district already has state approved special education facilities, the intermediate district board may establish a contract with this local district to provide services to nonresident pupils whom the intermediate board has assigned to the district. When there is no local district willing (and able) to provide needed services, the intermediate board may establish and operate such classes or services as needed. In a large number of intermediate districts, the voters elect to pay extra taxes sufficient to cover all special education costs not paid by the state.

This present legislation is the result of original legislation in 1954 which permitted certain counties to levy extra millage for special education and later amendments to include all counties in the state. An act in 1963 established the intermediate district concept (as opposed to a purely county basis) and further improved and extended the original enactment of 1952. Statewide acceptance of this method of assistance for special education has been quite good; local control has been maintained through the requirement of a majority vote favoring this financial plan.

Since initiation of this plan, a total of nearly 500 blind or deaf children has been enrolled in local school programs, thus saving the cost of building two new state residential institutions, and also permitting the children to remain in their own homes—where they should be if at all possible. In other words, the program has been economically practical in addition to being educationally sound. In the view of most evaluations, the intermediate district plan for special education in Michigan is quite satisfactory.

In summary, cooperative ventures in special education can and do work. The only question for any particular state is: which plan will work best here?

V
Problem Areas in Special Education Administration

THE day-to-day problems of the special education administrator are not too much different from those of many other school administrators. However, since most special education administrators report to a superintendent or an assistant superintendent (who in turn reports to the board of education), they do tend to miss the "pleasures" involved in the superintendent's more direct responsibility to the public for such items as property tax increase, the win-loss record of the football team, and perhaps even some of the books in the school library.

Lest it seem that the special education director misses too much of the "good life," it must be mentioned that he, too, has his areas of special challenge. A study of thirteen western states in *Administrative Problems in Special Education* by Wisland* considered the following problem areas:

1. Education of the public
2. Professional personnel
3. Student personnel
4. Communications
5. Administration policies and procedure
6. Supervision
7. Financial
8. Self-directed study and research

These major areas were broken down into sub-areas and various possible problems were investigated. Within the "education of the public" area, the problem ranked first by directors and supervisors of special education was that concerned with developing understanding and support for the special education program.

---

* Milton V. Wisland, doctoral dissertation, Colorado State College, 1962.

Within the "professional personnel" area, the problem of obtaining adequately trained personnel was ranked first. In the area of "student personnel," the concern for adequate provision for all types of exceptional children was the major difficulty.

In the "communications" area, the problems of helping parents understand their exceptional child seemed to be number one in importance. In the "administrative" area the problem of long-range plans was of major concern.

Under the category of "supervision," the problem of how to develop new programs and services to expand the program for exceptional children was ranked first. Under "finance," the problem of insufficient state aid was ranked highest, while in the problem area of "self-directed study and research" the leading concern was adequate time to carry out research.

When the data were analyzed independent of major area classifications, it was determined that the two major problems (according to the directors and supervisors questioned) were obtaining adequately prepared personnel and providing adequately for all types of exceptional children.

Obviously, the second major problem is closely related to the first and both are related to available finances, general philosophical support of special education and, more specifically, to the local school board and local superintendents' understanding of, and dedication to an educational program for exceptional children.

Probably the best overview of the total range of problems facing the administrator of special education may be found by reviewing a study completed in 1960 by the Los Angeles County Schools. In 1959, the superintendent of schools, city of Los Angeles, recommended to the board of education that funds be allocated to study the ". . . definition, function, organization, and administration of a special education program." There are few school systems large enough to feel they can justify expenditure of time and funds for a study of this nature. Among those few there is so much to be done in all of the various areas, it is truly amazing that this extremely useful, comprehensive study ever reached completion. The entire text of Chapter IV of the report entitled, "Summary, Conclusions, and Recommendations," is included as *Appendix* A to this text. This report was written for the Los Angeles schools, so that conclusions are reached which apply specifically to that city. However, the broad scope of this questionnaire study, its excellent design, and its uniqueness in the field of special education administration makes it a "must" for the educator's reading list.

Though the entire summary of this report is available as *Appendix A,* a general review of the problems under investigation would be of value at this point.

One major question relates to the definition of special education. For a state or local system to initiate and develop a meaningful, comprehensive special education program, there must be some sort of agreement as to what exceptionalities are included, and the specific definition of each exceptionality.

A *second major problem* relates to method of diagnosis and responsibility for pupil placement. Very often this is controlled to a certain extent (for the local school) by state regulations connected with state financial reimbursement. In establishing norms or guidelines in this area, provisions for exceptions to the rule are almost as important as the basic rule.

A *third major problem* has to do with class organization, housing, and transportation. Though these are separate problems, class organization determines housing needs to a considerable extent; *where* pupils are housed greatly influences transportation needs and costs. There is considerable philosophical disagreement among special educators regarding housing practices, but with very little research basis for any one point of view.

A *fourth major problem* is class size, and pupil or client load for such personnel as speech therapists and psychologists. Obviously this problem has considerable financial ramifications.

A *fifth major problem* is articulation of promotion and graduation policies and practices. This will vary greatly with the various exceptionalities.

A *sixth major problem* relates to the place of special education in the administrative framework. This will vary more by size of system than by any other single factor.

Also included in the Los Angeles report is a list of unsolved "dilemmas." These include: integration vs. segregation; specialized services vs. time-distance factor, generalist vs. specialist; occupational-vocational educational training vs. academic educational training; line vs. staff relationships for the special education program, and a static vs. a dynamic educational program.

A review of the discussion of the "dilemmas" will be most worthwhile to the special education administrator and the general school administrator.

Another way to look at sub-problems within any broad area of education is to attempt to divide them into the "everyday" problems of a very practical and immediate nature, as against the more theoretical or philosophical problems which may receive more sporadic attention. For example, everyday problems might include how to obtain substitute teachers for the absent special education teacher, or what to do with the teacher who just won't cooperate. Another "usual" problem is the boy who must be transported to get to the class where he can be served educationally, but who cannot tolerate school bus rules, endangers the safety of other passengers, and who lives with only one working parent who cannot arrange to transport him, or have him transported. Or there is the lower-borderline, educable mentally retarded girl who is pregnant and claims it happened during the afternoon activities period.

The theoretical-type question might be: Should the director of special education have direct line responsibility (upward) to the superintendent? Or should he report through the assistant superintendent in charge of instruction, or the deputy superintendent responsible for professional personnel? Or: Should we have one central special education school, or classes dispersed throughout the district? Any of these questions might be answered in a number of ways, and, in actuality, the answer would most likely be determined by the realities of the local situation. Local school system politics, or the prejudices of the superintendent and/or the board of education would probably determine the answer to the first question better than any theoretical supposition. As for the location of classes, the availability of facilities for housing special classes would have more weight in this decision than either theory or any preconceived notions, regardless of whether or not the questions are philosophically oriented.

On the other hand, it is necessary to have some theoretical and philosophical beliefs as a basis for day-to-day decisions which must be made, and for long-range planning. (In relation to these questions, it must be remembered that school attendance patterns and boards change—so don't give up!)

Therefore, it is essential for any administrator to have a fairly well-defined set of long range goals, plus some definite plans to implement these goals. It is also most necessary to have a set of guidelines whereby the day-to-day decisions can be made with some consistency. It is difficult to predict the kind of questions or problems which may arise with relation to special education curriculum, but the special educator must have a structure of final goals for boys and girls which can serve to guide decisions relating to specific curriculum problems as they arise. He must also have sufficient knowledge of state law, reimbursement requirements, local district policies, and other similar limiting or guiding factors in order to perceive almost immediately their relationships to various problems as they arise.

The two problem areas which would probably require more time than any other are, first, professional personnel problems, and second, pupil personnel problems. Finding teachers; keeping teachers; improving teacher techniques; dealing with teacher-pupil, teacher-parent, teacher-principal, or teacher-teacher relationships take a great deal of time. Working with pupils in such areas as identification of needs, placement, promotion, transportation, behavior problems, curriculum modification and pupil accounting also requires much time. In the very largest of school systems, the top special education administrator may do somewhat less of this direct dealing with professional personnel and pupils, but he will surely be dealing with the persons who must handle these problems.

As in any other problem situation, objectiveness, common sense, the ability to collect and organize facts (and sort out prejudices or hysteria), plus a reasonably good background of general knowledge in the area involved, will go a long, long way. Problems are "par for the course." The good administrator must simply play the game like the professional he claims to be.

VI

Growing Interest in Special Education Administration

IN the broad field of education, interest in a particular area or sub-area may usually be traced by six or seven indices. A first such index of interest is the number of full-length texts published in the area. A second index is the number of articles in professional journals which relate to this specific field. A third is the number of pamphlets, reports, and monographs published by state or national governmental agencies. A fourth is the number of dissertations completed in the sub-area in question.

A fifth index of interest is the number of statewide, regional, or national organizations with membership limited to the particular educational speciality under consideration.

A sixth, and quite different type of indicator, is the number of colleges and universities offering training programs in the sub-area. (Closely related to this index is the Federal support given to the sub-area in question. When the Government offers fellowships and scholarships, the universities quickly "develop" programs.)

A seventh, and sometimes not-too-reliable index, is the number of individuals employed in the specialty under consideration. This index is not always reliable because, as in the case of school superintendents, added interest may result in school reorganization, which in turn may result in fewer individuals employed.

If the seven indices just mentioned are carefully reviewed with relation to interest in the sub-area of administration of special education, the following general results will be found:

1. There is, at time of completion of this text, one text in this area.

2. There have been more articles pertaining to administration

of special education in professional journals in the last five years than in the preceding fifty years.

3. There have been more pamphlets, reports, monographs, etc., in the last ten years, than in the preceding fifty years.
4. Dissertations relating directly to special education administration have just begun to appear. (These have been greatly stimulated by the flow of doctoral students on very excellent United States Government fellowships.)
5. The Council of Administrators of Special Education (CASE) was affiliated with the Council for Exceptional Children in 1953. This division of the CEC which is a department of the National Education Association (NEA) is the first organization of special education administrators, and is growing steadily.
6. Colleges and universities have attempted to develop special education programs in an almost desperate manner since about 1958. It was at about this time that Federal fellowships made it most interesting (financially profitable) for such programs to develop. This crash-program development has not in every instance led to quality, but crash-programs are not noted for promoting quality.
7. There has been an increase in the number of directors of special education in the past five years which is proportionately greater than the increase in general school population. This increase is difficult to interpret, however, because many so-called "directors of special education" are dual jobs; with definite and specific standards, they would never stand the light of careful scrutiny.

The overall conclusion after consideration of these seven indices must be that there is definite evidence of growing interest in the function of the special education administrator.

Undoubtedly the reason for such growing interest relates to mounting evidence that:

1. There are many exceptional children in the United States who desperately need some sort of special educational programming and are receiving no help at all.

2. There is a similarly large number who are receiving inadequate or inappropriate help.
3. The quality of program often relates directly to both the adequacy of the local special education organization and to the quality of special education administrative leadership. It was precisely this realization which led to enactment of Public Law 85-926 and subsequent amendments (see *Appendix B*).

Historically, it may be noted that for a number of years following the turn of this present century, most of the school systems in the United States which made specific special educational provisions were able to administer and supervise these programs with a minimum of specially trained, supervisory help. Generally, they were administered by the director of elementary education or director or assistant superintendent in charge of instruction (in larger systems) and by "no-one-at-all" in smaller systems. In any event, teachers were left to their own devices, and placement practices were generally quite inadequate.

Fortunately, things have changed in more recent years. A number of things have led to this improvement. One factor has been genuine interest and, at times, inspired leadership from the Federal level. A second factor has been excellent leadership from a number of colleges and universities which have developed as centers of interest and influence in the education of the exceptional child. A third force has been a number of nationwide charitable organizations which have promoted both research and legislation relating to the exceptional child. A fourth influence has been the further evolution of the philosophy of American education which says, in effect, that "every child deserves an opportunity to develop his particular potentialities." Add to these forces, the growing influence of the Council for Exceptional Children, the interest of the late President John F. Kennedy, the impact of the Elementary and Secondary Education Act of 1965, and it becomes abundantly clear that special education is here to stay.

Though some colleges and universities would probably deny it, there were actually no doctoral level programs to train administrators of special education prior to the 1950's. It was at this time that Federal fellowships in this area became a possibility, then a reality. There were individuals receiving the Ph.D. or Ed.D. degrees in education, or educational psychology, or perhaps even in special education, who were beginning to administer special education programs, but the emphasis was on some sub-area of the field, with (maybe) some slight training in administrative skills and practices.

In very recent years, in recognition of the need for administrators who are properly trained to serve in this unique position, a number of better programs have been developed. The Office of Education has recognized these programs and is offering further encouragement in the form of grants to promote this type of development. There is a long way to go, but at least a start has been made.

There are a number of reasons why strong, competent local leadership is required in special education. One reason is the newness of the field. There is not the research background information which is available in many other areas of education. It is much easier (in special education) to do the wrong thing, and not have the mistake quickly recognized. Obviously, if there is not adequate supporting research data, quality leadership should help gather and interpret such data.

Another factor which dictates the need for top-flight leadership is the lack of agreement as to the "boundaries" of special education. It could be just as serious an error to attempt to serve too wide a range of needs, as to retain too narrow a band of responsibility. Enlightened leadership from within special education should play a major role in defining the scope of special education responsibility without yielding to the pressure of the enticement of Federal money or any other such influence.

A study of the development of programs of special education on a state-by-state basis, provides strong evidence that where there has been effective, competent leadership in a number of local systems and at the state level, the carry-over effect to the rest of the state has been considerable. Where there are only two or three good local programs and little state leadership, it is difficult to obtain helpful legislation or to influence other local systems in the direction of good, special educational services for girls and boys.

Finally, even if there is good legislative provision for special education, with good state-level leadership, without first-rate local leadership, the system falters and produces inferior results. Good special education programming does not "just happen"—it requires good leadership.

VII

Duties of the Local Special Education Administrator

THERE have been a number of studies relating to the duties of the special education administrator. In general, except for the relative scope of these studies, the end results have been quite similar. In the following discussion, "duties" and "competencies required of" the special education administrator will not be set apart, although they might well be separately delineated. Whenever possible (and appropriate) duties will be described, closely followed by a description and discussion of the competencies required to carry out these duties. It is hoped that this will provide for easy reading and a greater degree of brevity than a method which utilizes separate listing of duties and required competencies.

GENERAL ADMINISTRATIVE DUTIES

It is likely that a majority of special education administrators spend one-fourth or one-half of their time on what might be called general administrative duties and responsibilities. These are activities which they may lament as "lost hours" when it comes to promoting a better special education program, but are they really lost hours? Among the tasks involved here we might find the director of special education reviewing requisitions for curriculum material or equipment; preparing the budget for the following year; getting the wheels in motion for preparation of reimbursement claims; meeting with the superintendent's cabinet; meeting with the director of elementary education regarding additional class space needs for next year; consulting with parents or with visiting educators; meeting with the architects relative to special education needs in a building being planned; meeting with university officials regarding staff needs or the undergraduate training programs; interviewing teacher applicants; meeting with state officials about proposed legislation; determining class placement for children, or any of a hundred similar day-to-day responsibilities. It is true that many of these appear to be uninspiring tasks which may cause the director to wonder whether he should have ever left the classroom. It is equally true that many administrators never learn what tasks to delegate to subordinates, to other professional educators, or to secretarial and clerical help. However, the sum total of these daily events is the foundation on which a good program is built. Certainly the learning process which teaching allegedly promotes is the most important single function of the public schools, but without planning for future programs, without budgeting for additional classes, and even (incredibly) without the approval of requisitions and work-orders, the teaching process cannot move forward smoothly, and the learning process is hampered. If one of the major responsibilities of the administrator is to "open doors" so the learning process may proceed, these mundane "administrivia" are important when viewed as a correlated whole.

To carry out his administrative duties properly, the director must first understand the total functioning of the school system in which he works. This means understanding official line-staff relationships, and the additional "power-structures" which may be superimposed on the carefully charted, well-written relationships to be found in the policies and regulations handbook.

He must further be intimately acquainted with the various individuals and agencies in the community which contribute or relate to services for handicapped youth. In addition, he must understand how state leadership in special education influences the local program.

It is a good plan for the local administrator to become involved in an unofficial but active coalition with other directors in his state who serve districts of approximately the same size. This group can meet several times each year to discuss and plan action relative to recruiting, attempting to influence legislation, pressuring nearby colleges and universities relative to needed new courses, or perhaps just to find a sympathetic soul with whom to talk. Other members of the group can serve as a sounding board for proposed new programs or revisions of existing ones.

In addition to certain specific understandings and knowledge, the director must be able to handle detail, relate well with other educators, be fair, patient, understanding—and when necessary, know how to be quite positive and "hard-nosed."

SUPERVISORY DUTIES

To have an effective program, the local director of special education must supervise those individuals who report directly to him. In addition he must assist in supervision of such personnel as special education teachers (who report directly to their building principal); speech therapists (who may report to a chief therapist in larger systems) and others. With the responsibility of recommending the employment of individuals to fill specific vacancies, there is also the responsibility to supervise, evaluate and sometimes to recommend dismissal. The saying, "Those who would hire, must also fire," applies here. However, for the most part, professional personnel can be assisted in doing a better job; dismissals should be few and far between. An effective administrator is careful in selecting personnel, so that his major job becomes that of assisting potentially capable individuals to reach their full capabilities.

The author has followed a practice (in employment) of attempting to make certain that teacher candidates have good mental health, a realistic and meaningful philosophical outlook regarding special education, and a genuine respect for individual children. These considerations seem to be more important than the technical teaching competencies of the teacher, although the ideal combination is to find both proper attitudes and a high degree of technical skill and knowledge. In any event, a teacher with adequate intelligence, good attitudes, and mediocre teaching skill can be improved through experience and inservice training. However, a teacher with excellent technical knowledge of teaching, but with a sarcastic or ill-tempered approach to children is one who should not be hired in the first place.

RESEARCH AND CONTINUED PROFESSIONAL STUDY

Although relatively little time is spent by most special education administrators in pursuit of further professional competency via the professional study and/or research route, this is indeed an important duty and responsibility. In large systems, this goal may be attained by encouraging supervisors of various areas to pursue research, and by keeping them supplied with all available new texts, research reports and other materiel. Also, with the advent of the director of research in many larger school systems, part of this function can be served through this individual. If the administrator actually spends 5 per cent of his time in professional study and research, this is probably "par for the course."

PUBLIC RELATIONS ACTIVITIES

It has been said that the best public relations program (for a school) is an excellent educational program, and this is undoubtedly true. Most of the efforts of the person in charge of special education are directed toward the best possible program, and therefore toward public relations. But is that enough? Probably not.

The *very* best public relations program is an excellent educational program, plus planned efforts to keep the public adequately informed regarding educational provisions and opportunities for exceptional children in the schools.

The director of special education must not only be continually aware of the public-relations implications of everyday happenings in special education, but must also attempt to keep all special education personnel aware of their public relations responsibilities.

Within the limitations of local district regulations regarding contacts with news media, a concentrated effort should be made to keep the public informed. Local parent-teacher groups, sororities, service clubs, and similar groups, are always in need of speakers. The administrator, or other special education personnel, should be readily available to serve in this capacity. State and national publications, both in general and special education are interested in new and innovative programs, research, or special interest ideas.

If the director works actively at this project, the entire special education staff can become involved in a public relations effort which will pay generous dividends.

LEGISLATIVE RESPONSIBILITIES

It is imperative for the local director of special education to be fully aware of both state and federal laws pertaining to exceptional children. School laws express the feelings of lawmakers of the state and form the framework for the organization of special education, for its financing and for its administration. If it becomes apparent that laws are outdated and that the general public would likely support more advanced legislation which would be compatible with present-day thinking, the special educator must help lead the move for new laws. To do this, he must know how the legislative process works in his state, and what individuals or groups to see to start the process toward consideration of new legislation. It is a very real and highly important responsibility of the special education administrator to know and understand existing laws, be well aware of the legislative process, and lead the way to any additional legislation or to revisions of existing legislation. He can best fulfill these responsibilities if he keeps abreast of legislative developments in other states, is aware of various examples of "model legislation," and is astute enough to be able to sense the readiness of the general public and the lawmakers in his state. If the public or state legislators are not ready for needed changes, it is foolish to try to bulldoze them through. It is equally foolish just to wait for readiness to develop through some magical evolutionary process. Readiness for new concepts can be promoted with the public, just as reading readiness for children can be promoted. This requires some good basic information, a well-organized plan and enough motivation to supply the energy to carry the job through.

Legislative knowledge and planned efforts to correct any deficiencies in existing laws are an important part of the total responsibility of the special education administrator. He need not be a politician (in the sense of promoting partisan politics), but he should understand the political scene, and play the legislative game carefully, with deliberation.

STAFF DEVELOPMENT: INSERVICE TRAINING

There are many aspects to the staff development responsibility of the special education administrator. In most respects it is no different than the corresponding responsibility of other school administrators. This may involve provision of professional resource material; provision of opportunities for attendance of state level, regional and national professional meetings; establishment of local inservice meetings which really challenge the classroom teacher; arrangement for teacher participation in curriculum writing; selling the superintendent and the board of education on the need for specialized, full-time consultative help and other similar tasks. Most of these methods of promoting staff development would be reflected in additional budgetary support, particularly if the classroom teacher is relieved during the school day (by employing a substitute) to allow him to work on curriculum or attend all-day meetings.

In addition to these methods which may cost money and thus may be vetoed purely on the basis of cost, there are other methods which seldom call for additional fiscal support. The administrator can be a living example of one who keeps abreast of new developments, and by his example cause others to do the same. He can work with university officials to promote the offering of meaningful night, Saturday, or extension courses for special education teachers. He can demonstrate to the staff his open-mindedness and his desire to innovate, thus encouraging the use of new ideas, materials and other motivators. He can make every attempt to make inservice meetings come alive, even if he does not have the money to bring in nationally recognized leaders and authorities. He can work to bring building principals and other school district administrative personnel into the on-going training program, which may really "pay off." He can encourage teachers to participate in professional organizations, do action research, and become involved in other similar individual growth activities, by his strong support throughout the year, and by specific favorable comments about these activities at teacher evaluation time.

If the administrator is sufficiently motivated, the attitude will be contagious; the resultant better teaching will make boys and girls the final beneficiaries of this chain of events. This is the major goal of professional development efforts.

VIII
Special Education Leadership at the State Level

STATE leadership in special education can quickly make or break the educational program for exceptional children in all but the strongest school districts of the state. Because of the present stage of evolution in this field throughout much of the United States, this sub-area of education is much more susceptible to developmental retardation because of weak state leadership than most other sub-areas. This is due to both the heavy dependence of local districts on special education reimbursement and to the lack of information relating to special education on the part of many general administrators. Fortunately, this latter factor is being steadily improved and will continue to do so. As a result of these factors, it is most important that the state director of special education be a dynamic person with a good background in all phases of his field. One of the major problems to date, in many states, has been inadequate salaries for all educational leadership personnel at the state level. This, of course, applies to the position of state director of special education. A second problem has been a reluctance to employ specialized assistants (consultants) in the various disciplines represented on the total special education team.

Local directors of special education and university-level special educators must lead the way toward employment of strong, competent state directors.

The first state director of special education was employed in 1901, when an "inspector" to supervise special education became a member of the state department of education in one state. Today we have some person carrying a specific responsibility for the education of exceptional children (at the state level) in every state. The titles given these persons vary considerably, but the present trend is toward the "director" title for the person

80

who is in charge of the overall program as it relates to exceptional children. There also appears to be a trend toward calling the specialized personnel working in sub-areas (mental retardation, speech correction, school psychology), either "specialists" or "consultants." It would seem that either "director" or "assistant superintendent in charge of" is most appropriate for the top administrator, and that "specialist" or "consultant" is properly descriptive of the job of the special area personnel.

Various studies seem to indicate consensus regarding the idea that a state director must have very broad background and professional experience. In fact, it would appear nearly impossible to have all of the experience and training indicated as necessary by studies and statements of leadership persons in such groups as the Council of Administrators of Special Education (CASE).

It would appear that after broad general training at the post-master's level (including some course work in each of the major areas of special education), the best experience would be that of director of special education in a school district which provides for most exceptionalities. Then, an individual might be ready to be a state director.

There is a possible "fly in the ointment" here. In many states the state cannot compete salary-wise with the better school systems within its boundaries or in adjoining states. Where this situation applies, good persons may take the state directorship, but after becoming well-trained and demonstrating leadership, they are "picked off" by local school districts. The only solution to this dilemma is to raise the whole salary hierarchy at the state level.

In 1956, a report relating to state level special educators was published by the Office of Education. Though some time has passed since the publishing of this report, it remains an excellent summary of this important area of responsibility.

The following is quoted from Romaine P. Mackie and Walter E. Snyder (*Special Education Personnel in State Departments of Education,* Office of Education Bulletin No. 6, 1956, pages 7 to 16). The major responsibilities of the state director of special education are as follows:

Preparing the Budget

One of the chief duties of the administrator of a state program of special education is the preparation of the state budget for the education of exceptional children. While the specific duties may vary from state to state, the overall responsibility requires a complete familiarity with budgetary procedures in general and, in particular, the laws governing budgets in the state in which he works. The administrator must know the laws under which his budget will operate. In addition, he must know the laws governing the entire program of special education in order that he may prepare his budget in conformity with those laws as well.

Since budgets are drawn up in terms of estimated needs, the administrator should know the state program of special education so thoroughly that he can forecast financial requirements with a high degree of accuracy. He should be familiar with the costs of the various phases of the state program in order to evaluate the requests or "estimates of claim" which he receives and to fit them together in a total budgetary program for the state. He needs an intimate knowledge of the additional and varied costs of educating exceptional children and considerable familiarity with the general school laws of the state. For instance, some states reimburse school districts on the basis of excess costs. The cost varies widely according to the handicap suffered by the individual child, and the state director must be familiar with the variations. He must also be aware of the method by which basic costs are determined in the state and the variations in costs which occur from district to district.

Estimating needs is only part of the job in preparing a budget. The administrator should also be familiar with the sources of revenue and should balance his projected expenditures with his estimated income. While this may be controlled by statutory limitations in many cases, it is often determined by need as presented by the administrator. In the latter case, the administrator should be able to prepare a sound budget; he may also find himself faced with the necessity of defending it, a responsibility which requires him to have the personal characteristics set forth in an earlier part of this report.

Evaluating Legislation

Although many states have well-drawn laws governing the program of education for exceptional children, most of them are being amended from time to time to keep them abreast of new developments and needs. Also being drafted and presented for legislative consideration are new laws, some of which are good and some of which are of questionable value.

One of the greatest tasks of the administrator of a state program is to help in the passage of sound legislation and to discourage or forestall the passage of unsound legislation. Here again tact, judgment, leadership ability, and sometimes courage are needed in abundance. Specifically, however, the administrator should have a sound knowledge of the needs of all types of exceptional children in order to plan an effective legislative program which he believes will adequately meet these needs. Among other things, this would imply a comprehensive knowledge of legal provisions for special education in other states and familiarity with the operation of programs under those laws. In this way, he can better judge the merits of his proposals and can evaluate his efforts at improving legislative provisions. Complete and up-to-date knowledge of developments in each field of special education will help him to recognize legal changes necessary to permit a state to set up a functional program. He should be able to recognize the danger of too-great specificity in law and the advantages of flexibility under regulation.

Occasionally, legislation is introduced which, if passed, might result in tremendous financial or educational waste. The state administrator should be alert to detect such legislation, well enough informed to pick out its flaws, and competent to guide the sponsors into more constructive efforts. To be able to promote sound legislation and to advise against unsound provisions requires a knowledge of legislative procedures in practice, and competence as a statesman. The administrator should be able to appear before legislative committees and to present effectively the case for or against specific legislation and to muster the necessary support to carry the point.

Distributing State Funds

When workable laws are in operation and proper budgetary provisions have been made, a person from the state department of education should be given the responsibility of distributing state funds to local programs. In order to facilitate this procedure, the person responsible (usually the director) should be able to devise forms which will accomplish their aim with a minimum of inconvenience to the local district.

To avoid the charge of "red tape," the state worker should recognize the irritations which excessive reporting causes and should be able to keep his forms sufficiently clear and brief to minimize the charge, yet sufficiently detailed to keep within the law and the policies under which his department operates. To do these things he should have knowledge of the legal procedures involved, skill in streamlining and simplifying his procedures.

After the forms have been filled out and returned to the central office, the director should be prepared to evaluate them in detail and to pass upon their validity. Here, too, a knowledge of the law and of the regulations governing the program and of the detailed operation of local programs throughout the state is essential. When the director receives requests he cannot fill without deviating from state laws and regulations, he should be able to turn them down without antagonizing the petitioner and without appearing to be critical or dictatorial. Personal qualities, coupled with sound knowledge of state and local programs, are essential to successful performance of these duties.

Fostering and Improving Local Programs

Most states in which special education programs function have recognized through their laws the advantages of local control and responsibility. A major duty of state personnel, however, is the fostering of local programs and the improvement of those programs. In order to carry out this duty, these workers should have arrived at a sound philosophy of special education in terms of which they can evaluate programs in operation. Such a philosophy will have been developed out of a program of training in general, as well as in special education and through practical experience as a worker in the field.

In all states, some local areas continue to go unserved, either because of lack of local leadership or lack of funds. To help such districts, the state workers should be competent to arouse their interest, to create a desire for local services, and to help them evaluate their needs. Assisting the community with such an evaluation requires knowledge and skill in organization, competencies in the various fields of specialty and leadership in group dynamics. The preparation of forms for the evaluation of community needs requires a knowledge of research techniques and the ability to collect and interpret data.

Local programs, because of various factors, frequently become overbalanced in one direction or another. The director should be able to see such disparities in operation and help the local workers reinstate a proper balance between the various segments of their program. The need for other improvements will often become apparent; these will also require skill on the part of the state leaders in bringing them into more effective working order. It is important to accomplish these changes effectively but without dictation or force. State laws and regulations must be interpreted, cooperation must be secured and professional relationships must be established. While considerable knowledge is required, the success of the undertaking will also depend upon understanding, judgment, discrimination, and the ability to cultivate good interpersonal relationships.

Establishing Standards

Standards for the evaluation of local educational programs for exceptional children must be established and must be kept under continuous study and review. Especially in states where funds for education of exceptional children are reimbursed from the state treasury to the local school district, are specific methods of determining eligibility for state support necessary. The state director has a leadership responsibility in the development of such standards. He should have a thorough knowledge of the techniques of specialized instruction, the criteria for the diagnosis and placement of handicapped and gifted pupils, the desirable size of classroom, the physical facilities, and the special instructional devices needed for the education of children within each type of handicapping condition. He should be able to synthesize this knowledge into a set of principles which will guide the development of standards for local programs.

Since all standards include statements on the qualifications of teachers of exceptional children, the state administrator should have a working knowledge of teacher education facilities, of the course requirements of programs for teachers of each type of exceptional child, and of teacher certification procedures in the various states.

Recruiting Teachers and Cooperating in Teacher Education

Since the supply of properly prepared teachers in the field of special education is especially limited, the state director should participate actively both in recruitment efforts and in the preservice education of teachers. To be able to participate, he needs competence in the preparation of special education teachers and a knowledge of the essential preparation required of them. By knowing the goals, techniques, materials, and equipment needed in each special area, and particularly by being informed on recent developments and improvements, he can add to the effectiveness of the programs now in operation. He should have the ability to work with private and state-supported teacher education institutions in order to help them to improve their programs and should be able to evaluate fairly, accurately, and without bias the potentialities of institutions seeking to enter the field.

Encouraging Inservice Growth of Teachers

The inservice training of teachers in the field of special education is of major importance, both because of rapid technological changes and because of much inadequate training at the preservice level. Much of the work of the state personnel centers in the upgrading of teachers in service through extension and campus classes, teacher workshops in local school systems, and faculty meetings throughout the state. The state leader should be an effective "teacher of teachers" in order to bring to these meetings the inspiration and enthusiasm which will appeal to the group. He should be familiar with the latest materials and techniques of instruction and with the most up-to-date literature in each field. He should have access to and be familiar with modern research in the field of education and in medicine, physical therapy, and other disciplines bearing upon the education of handicapped children.

The administrator of a state program of special education should be adept at organizing workshops and other types of inservice meetings for special education personnel; and he should possess the skill, the enthusiasm, and the imagination necessary to make these meetings successful. He must have the ability to select, organize, and make available the teaching materials, mechanical and other, which will add to the growth of teachers on the job. Furthermore, he should be skilled in adult education in order to work with parent groups and in organizing workshops and other resources for parent education. Only to the extent that parents become partners with the schools, will the work of the special teachers reach its maximum goal.

Besides knowing the local facilities for preparing special education personnel, the state leader should be well informed on out-of-state resources for teacher education in order that he may give sound advice to those seeking specialized preparation and may guide them to the best programs for their particular needs.

Supervising Education in Residential Schools

Increasingly, states are recognizing that the program of education for exceptional children is a total one and that it should be directed by educational personnel. As a result, the responsibility for the operation of residential facilities for the blind and deaf is, in many states, being shifted from institutional to state department of education agencies. With this transition have come certain new responsibilities for the state director of special education. In order to carry his responsibilities, the state director of special education should know the educational needs of handicapped children and the services available in day and residential schools sufficiently well to set up effective evaluative procedures for selective placement of children.

In order to be accepted in a leadership role as the coordinator and, perhaps, administrator of *all educational services* for the handicapped children of a state, the state director should have intimate knowledge of educational programs, in both day and residential schools for exceptional children. Since the operation of residential schools involves housing, feeding, and caring for children twenty-four hours a day, the state director should understand the problems involved and their relationships to the educational program.

There is increasing evidence that educational programs of the residential schools are becoming more closely geared to public school programs in an effort to better serve the needs of the handicapped child. The state administrator should understand the need for freer interchange of pupils between these two educational units and work as a liaison person to facilitate the free transfer of pupils to best meet their needs. To do so, he should be able to convince the public school administrator and teacher of the feasibility of educating selected children with handicapping conditions in the day school classes, and at the same time cooperate with residential school personnel in providing for those who require twenty-four-hour care. If he himself is convinced of the soundness of the program he espouses, he should have the courage to put it into operation and the leadership qualities necessary to make it work.

From his training and experience, the state worker should be familiar with the many problems encountered by those boys and girls, a large part of whose childhood and youth is spent in a residential school environment—the comparative isolation from the world, the often limited social contacts, the sometimes routinized program, and the long periods of separation from family and close friends. Understanding these, the state worker should know what needs to be done to better the circumstances, and how to work with residential personnel in order to lessen the unfortunate conditions which sometimes exist in residential schools.

Many excellent examples could be cited throughout the country in which every effort is being made to make the residential school a real home for the child. Such schools perform a highly useful function which today can be performed by no other agency.

Maintaining Interagency Relationships

In every state and in every community, many individuals and agencies, both public and private, are interested in and working for the exceptional children of the area. Among them are social, educational, medical, and health agencies whose overlapping responsibilities and interests sometimes unknowingly work to the disadvantage of the child, rather than to his advantage. Some leadership must be available if these various interests are to avoid serious overlappings, omissions, or inefficiency. Frequently the state director of special education is in the most strategic position to serve as the coordinating link between these various services. Accurate knowledge and leadership ability, together with tact, patience, wisdom, and judgment are again essential. Even more, perhaps, the state worker should be capable of objectivity and be free from prejudices. He should understand human nature and the motivations which lead to action in certain directions rather than in others. He should be especially well informed on the goals and objectives of the various agencies at work and their methods of operation, so that he can best serve the handicapped children of his state.

Preparing Publications

As leader of the educational program for exceptional children in his state, the director should coordinate, edit, and prepare for distribution a wide variety of publications in various areas of special education. While the writing may often be delegated to others, the final responsibility is his, and he should be equipped to deal with it. He should be able to recognize the need for certain types of materials and select those which he and his staff have the ability to prepare. He should be able to organize and plan the content of such publications, to edit the material, to advise and encourage the writer, and at times even participate in the writing. This work requires proficiency in organization, composition, syntax, and other skills necessary in producing a finished product which is interestingly written, technically accurate, and grammatically correct.

Selecting and Directing Personnel

In many programs of special education, there is at the state level a corps of assistants, each of whom is a specialist in a certain area of exceptionality. In order to select these assistants, the state director should be a good judge of men and women, and should be able to develop adequate criteria upon which to base his selections. The ability to draw up such criteria requires a sound knowledge of each area of specialization and of the competencies needed by workers in each field. He should know the kinds of services which the worker will be expected to perform and the qualities needed in order to perform those services effectively.

Furthermore, he should be able to select staff members who will work together as a team in order that they may make each area complement the other in developing a well-rounded program. If his state does not have a civil service system, he should have the courage to resist political pressures in making his appointments and be willing to resist any effort to let appointments be made other than on merit.

When his corps of assistants is assembled, the director should possess the personal qualities of leadership which will enable him to weld the group into an effective, dynamic organization. He should be able to delegate authority and to hold the group to high standards of performance, allowing freedom for ingenuity and individuality, yet keeping the entire group devoted to the accomplishment of clearly and sharply defined goals.

Sponsoring and Directing Research

The administrator should be an expert consumer of research and, at times, an active participant in research projects. He should keep abreast of current research findings as they relate to the education of exceptional children, and should have sufficient understanding of research methodology to evaluate the validity and significance of such studies.

The state leader has a role to play in the establishment of continuing active research programs which are likely to give local communities and the state accurate knowledge of the needs, of the validity of established or proposed procedures, and of the success of various programs. He should open avenues of communication which will lead to joint research undertakings; he should encourage the interest of university personnel and research foundations in the problems most pressing of solution and most fruitful of investigation.

A "number 13" should be added to this excellent list. Because of the arrival on the scene of the Elementary and Secondary Education Act, and its resultant effect on special education, the state director *must* become an expert in assisting local districts in using ESEA funds for handicapped children. This means he must be intimately acquainted with this Federal legislation and must make certain that local superintendents and directors of special education utilize all of the various provisions. This will likely mean more bulletins, more meetings, and more time spent in personal contacts, but the "payoff" for boys and girls is tremendous.

Although a great many additional words could be used in attempting to emphasize the importance of the state directorship, or to list responsibilities in another manner, it is appropriate to say that the state director must possess those qualities of leadership which are prerequisite to success in all professions which involve meeting and working with the public. This particular job involves meeting with and relating to an unusually wide range of individuals, from parents (who may or may not be politicians) to politicians (who may or may not be parents). Some are representing the needs of their children, others are mainly "guarding tax dollars." All must be handled with tact and understanding, but without losing sight of either the actualities of life, or the dreams and vision which may lead to better educational programs for children and adolescents.

Diplomacy, tact, maturity, adjustability, judgment, breadth of knowledge—all these and more are required in this highly important job.

IX

The Role of Other Professionals in the Community

THE MEDICAL DOCTOR

THE importance of the role of the medical doctor is often overlooked by the special educator, to the detriment of the child as well as the program of special education. It may be granted that some physicians, when asked by anxious mothers, give too hasty answers relating to education or educational programming. However, the majority of physicians are more than willing to cooperate fully with provisions for special educational planning, if educators play their role properly. Many noncommittal answers may be given to the questioning parent, either because the medical doctor is unsure of the answer or because he does not want to risk taking a direction of thinking which may be different from that proposed at school. It is of the utmost importance that the special educator *actively seek the help and cooperation of the medical profession.* Doctors in specialty areas, such as those working with children with vision or hearing handicaps, are generally quite well informed about public school opportunities and private and state institutional facilities. These physicians are in contact with special education programs, and it is relatively easy to keep them well informed on the existence of local facilities. In many cases, they play an active role in developing facilities, or promoting orderly evolution of existing facilities.

The pediatrician and the general practitioner are in a somewhat different position. Parents, particularly mothers, have depended on "their doctor" through the preschool years as a sort of super-counselor and adviser, and the doctor is able to help the mother through most of her problems. Then suddenly, the questions relate to reading problems, general learning problems, or behavior problems and the mother confidently expects the same reassuring answers, and the solution, perhaps, in chewable, candy-coated, easy-to-take form.

What should the doctor do? He obviously cannot leave the parents without an answer. This is where school personnel must play their role.

If the school system has kept the medical profession informed as to all of its programs—special classes; remedial classes; services of school psychologists and counselors; transportation help for physically handicapped; desk model hearing aids; magnifiers, and all of the other special-purpose school programs, the doctor has an answer. *Equally important, or perhaps even more important, is having a school person whom doctors can contact or can tell parents to contact for advice and counsel.*

The medical doctor holds a unique place in the eyes of parents. More than one parent has been heard to say, "I sometimes get so mad at that man, but you know—he's right. I'll do what he says." With this position of nearly absolute authority, the doctor can be of tremendous help, particularly with parents who find it hard to face facts obvious to all but the parents.

In many states the doctor alone can certify need for a particular type of special equipment or special program. When it seems advisable to suggest referrals to state medical centers, the doctor is the key person. When apparent hearing loss is discovered at school, it is the doctor who can look into the possibility of remediation or referral to highly trained specialists.

When a child is disturbed and/or hyperactive, a doctor can prescribe medication. When school authorities note that a child on medication is apparently "losing ground," it is the doctor who will determine whether the parents are actually using the prescribed medication; if so, he may try a different dosage or a different prescription.

In many communities the local medical association selects a representative to work with school authorities as a sort of liaison person. If this is not a practice, it should be encouraged.

It should be noted that prevention of the various handicapping conditions is a major national concern. Tremendous strides have been taken by the medical profession in aiding the hard-of-hear-

ing, the visually handicapped and the orthopedically handicapped. Epilepsy has been controlled to an amazing degree
through medical research in the past twenty years.

A number of diseases and conditions which damage the brain
and result in mental retardation have been discovered, and steps
have been taken to prevent these conditions whenever possible.
Intricate methods of removing abnormal brain growths surgically
and the recent discoveries of faulty body chemistry involved in
diseases such as phenylketonuria and galactosemia, are but a
few examples of the medical wonders accomplished through the
dedicated work of medical researchers. Fifty years ago, RH blood
factor incompatibility led to retardation, which accounted for
approximately one out of every one hundred admissions to mental
institutions. This is now under almost complete control.

Members of the medical profession in the local community
are a key part of the special education team. Unlike others, the
time they take to be informed and to work jointly with educators
is not necessarily a part of their job and seldom results in additional remuneration. The administrator of a special education
program should spend some time in cultivating the friendship of,
and working with, the physicians in the community; he should
always be available to consult with, or send requested information
to the local physician, whichever seems necessary. In return, he
may expect things to go more smoothly, and the interests of
children with special educational needs to be better served.

THE VOCATIONAL REHABILITATION COUNSELOR

The vocational rehabilitation counselor can be a key person in
arriving at the goal of useful employment for handicapped individuals. For many years, crippled youth and adults have been
helped to find and keep suitable employment through the excellent efforts of this counselor. School personnel must maintain
close contact with the local representatives of vocational rehabilitation in order to plan effectively for physically handicapped boys and girls. However, this is only a small part of the
services to be received through the counselor.

In 1943, Public Law 113 was enacted. With its enactment,

individuals whose primary handicap was mental retardation became eligible for vocational rehabilitation services. Since 1943, there has been a steady growth of such services for the retarded by counselors in this field.

According to official records, during the years 1945-50 inclusive, 2,091 mentally retarded persons (MR's) were rehabilitated into gainful employment. In the years 1951-56 inclusive, a total of 3,628 MR's were rehabilitated.

In 1962, 3,562 MR's were rehabilitated (nearly as many as in the five-year period 1951-56) and over 6,000 retarded persons will be rehabilitated in 1966. This increase in service is just another of the significant happenings in the total area of aid for the handicapped.

As vocational rehabilitation service for the mentally retarded has grown, so has the need for a close-working relationship between public school special education personnel and vocational rehabilitation counselors. In larger cities, the regional director of vocational rehabilitation may see fit to assign one or more counselors to work full time in a cooperative effort with public school special education employees. In smaller communities, part-time assistance from such a counselor can be expected. The National Office of Vocational Rehabilitation has assumed a leading role in planning conferences and workshops designed to inform vocational rehabilitation counselors and special educators regarding their joint function and responsibilities.

The following remarks are from the keynote speech given at the Vocational Rehabilitation-Special Education Workshop held in May, 1966, at Gull Lake, Michigan. Dr. Daniel McAlees, coordinator of the Rehabilitation Counselor Training Program at Colorado State College, and President (1967-68) of the National Rehabilitation Counseling Association, was the speaker.

These sections summarize quite adequately the role of the vocational rehabilitation counselor in serving mentally retarded youth, and, in addition, reflect the way a vocational rehabilitation counselor views the public school special education program.

> The Vocational Rehabilitation program is made up of many services, each of which could be explored for issues dealing with the retarded. These services include:

1. Individual evaluation with medical, psychological, and social vocational assessments
2. Medical care and hospitalization
3. Artificial appliances with training to use them
4. Personal adjustment, prevocational and vocational training
5. Provision of maintenance during rehabilitation, including transportation costs
6. Occupational tools and equipment
7. Selective placement and follow-up in employment
8. Counseling throughout the process

The counseling services, including counseling of the family as it relates to the individual's rehabilitation plan, are the underlying foundation for the total program. The fields of education and vocational rehabilitation are fruitful major avenues for the stimulation of progress in work with the retarded for two major reasons. First, mental retardation is a disability which usually appears in childhood, highlighting the importance of education as a program of individual development. Second, the crucial years of early adulthood will set the patterns of adult living, highlighting the importance for vocacational rehabilitation to help the retarded make the transition from school, to work, and adult living. Although the program is called Vocational Rehabilitation, it believes completely in the significance of Habilitation. The difference in words should present no difference in meaning either to education or vocational rehabilitation.

Although we fully recognize the vast individual differences between the mentally retarded, making them a most heterogeneous group, I would like to propose a classification to serve as a practical guide to the personnel of vocational rehabilitation and education agencies as they work together. The classification guide is based on overall vocational prospects of retarded adolescents:

Directly Placeable Group from School to Job

This is composed of young adults for whom special education proves sufficiently effective as preparation for employment, and who may become employed in competitive jobs directly from school. These persons may be assisted in finding suitable employment by school counselors, employment services, family or friends, and the vocational rehabilitation counselor only in special cases.

Deferred Placeable Group Post-School Preparation to Job

These are young adults in need of additional services beyond those offered by the school. They need further preparation and assistance, such as prevocational and vocational experiences; physical or psychiatric evaluation; treatment; on-the-job training; counseling, or personal-adjustment training, before they may be placed in competitive employment.

Sheltered Employable Group

These are young adults who are capable of partial self-support in the carefully supervised environment of a sheltered workship, after preparation services beyond school.

Self-care (nonself-supporting group)

These include persons who may partially care for themselves in the home and be able to participate in a "social therapy center," but who are not capable of engaging in productive employment even in a sheltered workshop.

Preparation for Job Placement

The preparation of retarded youth for vocational placement is an extensive undertaking both in terms of time and subject matter. Implicitly, preparation begins in the child's preschool years where the family and community can exert a critical influence on his intellectual and personality development. It is during the child's school years, however, that he is introduced to the complex elements involved in socio-occupational adjustment.

The Role of Counseling in Preparation for Employment

Counseling is accepted as an integral part of the total program of education and vocational preparation of retarded adolescents. Effective counseling and guidance can occur through both formal and informal contacts with students, and thus all persons engaged in the education and habilitation of the mentally retarded have some degree of counseling responsibility.

Informal Counseling

Informal counseling occurs when the teacher takes advantage of incidental opportunities which arise in relation to classroom activities to assist students in coping with personal, social, academic or vocational problems. For example, during a unit on occupational information, a student may express an unrealistic vocational aspiration. The teacher, by providing the student with an opportunity to explore a broad range of possible occupational pursuits along with various job requirements is, in reality, engaging in informal counseling.

In most situations at the primary through the intermediate levels, the teacher will be the person of greatest influence in the personal and social development of the child, since he is the one who will develop the most intimate relationship with the student. The teacher is engaged in counseling to the extent that he deliberately promotes growth or works toward desirable modifications in the personal and social development of the child.

Much of the counseling of the teacher will be of the preventive type, inasmuch as he is in a strategic position to help insure that minor problems do not develop into more serious ones.

Formal Counseling

In contrast with the informal counseling carried on by the teacher within the classroom situation, formal counseling implies the services of professional persons with a specific background of training and experience in counseling and guidance who work in schools, or in rehabilitation agencies, or both. Formal counseling directed at the more complex problems presented by students requires skills and a background of training not usually held by the classroom teacher. It is therefore essential that the teacher have available for support and assistance the services of the rehabilitation counselor.

Even with respect to formal counseling, however, there must be close cooperation between the rehabilitation counselor and classroom teacher. The teacher is often able to complement the counselor's work by making it possible for the student to implement new values and principles of behavior acquired during counseling. The work of the counselor is often directly related, for example, to the academic performance of the student in the classroom.

The services of the rehabilitation counselor become an especially important adjunct to the school program for retarded adolescents where major personal, social and vocational problems arise as a result of the impending integration into employment and community living. Even with the more complex problems of this period, however, the teacher will be able to complement the work of the counselor. With some kinds of problems, a teacher's intimate relationship with a student may render his informal counseling very effective. An example of cooperation between counselor and teacher can be seen in the relationship between vocational counseling and a teaching unit on occupational opportunities. While the counselor is helping the student to achieve a realistic assessment of his abilities and limitations, the teacher is providing him with an opportunity of measuring these abilities against the requirements of specific jobs. It becomes increasingly essential, however, at the secondary school ages, that the skills and services of the teacher be supplemented by the provision of specialized services for vocational, personal, social, family, placement, and post-school follow-up counseling.

There probably will be many patterns by which schools and vocational rehabilitation agencies cooperate in meeting the counseling needs of mentally retarded students. The most effective pattern will probably depend on the resources of both the school and rehabilitation agency in the particular community, local conditions, and the particular needs of the students included in the program. In some situations, the school counselor may carry the responsibility quite far. In others, the rehabilitation agency may serve the school in a consultant capacity by assisting school personnel in charting the direction toward employment for individual students, and by providing the student with direct vocational rehabilitation services when needed. In other situations rehabilitation personnel may participate more actively in the school program by working and counseling directly with students, in addition to serving as a consultant to the teacher. In a few communities, the rehabilitation agency has assigned a staff member to work full time in cooperation with the schools in meeting the needs of students. Such a person may serve as an effective liaison between the school program and the services of the rehabilitation agency.

On-the-Job Training

The on-the-job training program is one of the outgrowths of the expansion of specialized public school programs. Finding that many mentally retarded adolescents were unable to maintain themselves in competitive employment upon termination of school attendance, many school systems have begun to develop extended school programs to age eighteen, and in some cases to age twenty-one. An integral feature of many of these extended programs has been the inclusion of on-the-job training designed to facilitate successful transition from school to employment.

In the on-the-job training program, the student usually spends part of a day or week in acquiring work experience and learning specific job skills. The remainder of his time is spent in school. A few programs have been organized so that the student spends full time for a period in the job training program, and then alternates this with a period of full-time school attendance. The nature of the work experience obtained in the job training program is, of course, dependent upon the prevailing economic conditions in the community, and the range of occupational opportunities available. Individual work experiences must take into consideration the ability of the employer to accept and be a positive factor in the development and training of the students.

A close liaison should be maintained between school and employer so that the student may receive careful supervision in the work experience program. Many schools accomplish this by appointing a counselor to work full time with student-workers, employers, and as a liaison with classroom teachers. In other schools, teachers' schedules are set so as to permit time for working with employers and observing their students on the job. Since employers and fellow employees vary so greatly in the demands they make, and in the manner in which they react to mentally retarded workers, it is desirable that students obtain several kinds of work experiences in the on-the-job training program.

Selective Placement

Carefully planned programs of vocational preparation of mentally retarded youth should be culminated by selective placement. Experience has shown that probability of successful adjustment is increased when students are given assistance in locating and adjusting to suitable jobs.

Selective placement is comprised of an extended sequence of activities which precede and follow actual job placement. These include evaluation, exploration of job opportunities, job placement, postplacement counseling, and other post-school services.

Evaluation

The objective of formal evaluation is to enable professional personnel to make a placement which will match the capacity and characteristics of the student with the demands of a particular job. It is essential that a thorough evaluation of the student be carried out well ahead of the time when actual job placement is to be made. The first aspect of evaluation is to determine the student's need for placement assistance. In some cases this assistance may not be immediately needed as, for example, when the student will be employed by, or through, a member of his own family. Those who do require placement assistance should undergo an evaluation to ascertain the nature of the placement services they will need. In this stage of evaluation, it would seem desirable that school personnel and the vocational rehabilitation counselor work together. Through their cooperative efforts they can determine whether the student should receive the services of a placement agency, such as the State Employment Service, or whether he should receive further training and/or remediation and preparation for a specific job through the Vocational Rehabilitation Agency. Where testing is required to determine the eligibility and feasibility for agency service, the rehabilitation counselor will be able to indicate the procedures for obtaining this service.

It should be recognized that, in many instances, student needs may change following termination of school attendance. For example, a student who has indicated that he has been promised a position with a friend or relative may find that the job does not materialize.

Another youth may show all the signs of needing only placement service and not training. With a trial period of employment it may become evident that he requires further rehabilitation service. Rehabilitation and special education should therefore make provisions for follow-up and periodic reevaluations of the services needed by a particular student.

Exploration of Job Opportunities

Explorations of job opportunities in the community should be a cooperative activity on the part of all agencies concerned with the vocational placement of the mentally retarded. These explorations should be coordinated so as to avoid repetitive, time-consuming interviews. In some communities this confusion has been avoided by the appointment of a coordinating committee which assumes responsibility for gathering all necessary occupational information and communicating it to the various agencies involved.

Information gathered in this way is used by each agency according to its needs. The school, for example, may use data on available job opportunities in revising its subject matter on occupational adjustment. In this way the subject matter of the classroom becomes more closely related to actual conditions in the community. Employment agencies can use this information for job classification and listing of services. This information is also used directly in working with those students who are ready for immediate job placement. Rehabilitation agencies can use this information in planning rehabilitation services that will be most appropriate to available job opportunities. In addition to knowledge of available job opportunities, vocational exploration can provide information concerning facilities and skills of the employer for training mentally retarded workers. This knowledge will be helpful to placement personnel in working out a plan for on-the-job training of the new worker.

Job Placement

Actual placement on the job can be most effectively achieved by careful preparation of student and employer. The actual placement will often be made by the agency most involved with the student. For example, a student who does not require special training prior to placement on a specific job may be served by the school itself. A student requiring such services as training, treatment, or prothesis, would probably be a client of the vocational rehabilitation agency for both the service and placement. In some cases, the schools may have an established backlog of jobs that have been used in the on-the-job training program. Where indicated, it might be advisable to permit certain students to extend their part-time experience into a full time job.

It was not the function of this report to go into a detailed description of jobs into which the educable mentally retarded can be placed. The usual lists of jobs reported as suited to retarded workers might be a somewhat outmoded and rather restricted sampling today. The rapid technological changes which are occurring are creating new job possibilities for the mentally retarded while some existing ones are being eliminated. The possibilities will vary considerably from one community to another, depending largely upon what kinds of businesses and industries happen to be located in a particular area. Community surveys conducted in an attempt to discover what kinds of work the mentally retarded might perform, have often turned up surprising possibilities which are not mentioned in the classic lists of job opportunities for the retarded.

Postplacement Counseling

Job placement should include plans for follow-up if optimal adjustment is to be achieved. Rehabilitation personnel have found that many seemingly minor incidents or misunderstandings can be ameliorated early in the employee's and employer's experience, thereby preventing undesirable consequences. A girl placed as a bus girl in a cafeteria, for example, interpreted her job to be that of only clearing tables and carting the dirty dishes to the dishwasher. By accident, a customer dropped a bowl of soup on the tile floor. When the manager asked the girl to mop up the debris in the interest of safety, she became confused and somewhat defensive, since she could not see the relationship between this request and her duties. She was about to make an issue of this simple incident, but fortunately decided to talk it over with her placement counselor, who helped her to see the logic in the assignment. Without assistance from a postplacement counselor this girl might have forced this minor event into a situation that cost her the job. It might possibly have closed this avenue for job placement for a long time to come for this girl as well as others.

The employee should be encouraged to discuss a wide range of problems, since many factors not directly related to employment can have an effect on job adjustment. Time should be taken to discuss the employee's work with the person who is the immediate supervisor. If there are deficiencies in the employee's work or adjustment, the counselor may be in a position to effect a favorable change in the employee. Rehabilitation personnel have found that it is often better and easier to counsel with an employer in order to maintain the worker on the present job, than it is to find a new job for him. In some instances, supervisors, in an attempt to reward good service, have unwittingly "promoted" their mentally retarded employees into jobs that were too complex. In one case, a mentally retarded youth was made foreman of a crew. Counseling with the supervisor would have prevented the resultant failure and avoided the frustration which occurred on the part of both employee and employer.

The foregoing remarks should convince special educators that for some of our special education "graduates," extended professional counseling is essential. These excerpts should also demonstrate the progressive and realistic way in which vocational rehabilitation views its responsibilities toward the mentally retarded. If the number of mentally retarded individuals rehabilitated (or habilitated) reaches eight thousand to ten thousand by 1970, as is expected, the cost of this service will be ten to twelve million dollars. Presuming that this service is worthwhile, and presuming that tax dollars for public education will not become much easier to obtain, it is certainly essential that special education administrators work with, and encourage the efforts of vocational rehabilitation.

X

What Every Special Educator Should Know

ORGANIZATIONS AND ASSOCIATIONS YOU SHOULD KNOW

ADMINISTRATORS of special education must be familiar with the various organizations which are related to their department in the public school. These organizations are important as a source of general information, and for specific research data; in many cases, they also provide valuable help in personnel procurement. They may have considerable influence on the development of university training programs and may, over a period of years, drastically affect certification requirements.

They serve as powerful pressure groups in representing the area of exceptionality they espouse, and may be of inestimable help in influencing both state and federal legislation. They provide a helping hand in accomplishing local goals, but if a special education director or superintendent appears to have forgotten certain exceptionalities, the groups primarily concerned with that exceptionality may be counted on to "sound off."

There are various categories of such organizations, but generally they fall into three main groups. First, there are groups composed, for the most part, of individuals who are not professionals in the field, but have sincere and sometimes "missionary" concern relating to their particular area. These groups obtain the active assistance of nationally recognized leaders in public office or industry, can wield considerable influence on state and national legislators. Their efforts are positive; they are generally cooperative with local boards of education. They sometimes want to move faster (in a specific situation) than is feasible, but whenever possible, the special education administrator should "play ball" with such groups. In the last analysis, however, a director or supervisor of special education is employed by the board of education, and serves under the superintendent of schools. His loyalty must remain with those who employ him.

A second general group is composed of organizations wherein membership is reserved for professionals in the particular field (e.g., American Psychological Association, American Speech and Hearing Association.) These groups have relatively more effect on such things as college and university training programs, state certification requirements, codes of ethics, proposed working conditions and similar matters.

A third group is actually a "grouping" of related organizations within a parent organization. This is the Council for Exceptional Children (CEC), one of the major subgroups of the National Education Association. There are, at the time of writing, eight divisions of the CEC which are outlined in the next paragraph. The CEC, through its total organization, and through its eight divisions, is a major force in shaping the direction of movement of special education in the United States and Canada today. In recent years, a significant number of excellent publications have come from the CEC, and more are on the way. The CEC, adding "muscle" to the Office of Education, has had major responsibility for much of the recent Federal legislation which has been so beneficial to special education. Called upon in an "advisory" capacity, the CEC has helped shape much of the recent reorganization in the areas related to exceptional children in the Office of Education. As you will note from membership requirements, the Council (and its divisions) invites membership from a broad group and is becoming a dominant organization in the field.

Following is a listing of the eight divisions of the CEC, the statement of purpose, the membership requirements of each. These divisions are completely autonomous, set their own dues, publish newsletters, plan their own programs. In each case, however, a person must first be a member of CEC in order to join a division.

The Council of Administrators of Special Education (CASE) affiliated with CEC in April, 1953. Its purpose is:

". . . to promote professional leadership, to provide opportunity for study of problems common to its members, and to communicate through discussions and publications information that will develop improved services for exceptional children."

CASE Membership Requirements: Active membership is open to anyone who (a) is a current member of the Council for Exceptional Children, and (b) administers, supervises, and/or coordinates a program or classes of special education for exceptional children in a local (city, county, or district) school system. (Principals of special schools or administrators teaching part-time are not eligible.)

The Teacher Education Division (TED) affiliated with CEC in April, 1953. Its purposes are:

". . . to stimulate and actively assist in the development and improvement of programs of professional preparation for teachers and other professional workers who serve exceptional children."

TED Membership Requirements: Membership is open to any member of CEC who subscribes to the purpose of the division and has a professional role in teacher education and/or research.

The Council for the Education of the Partially Seeing (CEPS) affiliated in May, 1954. Its purposes are:

". . . to bring about a better understanding of educational and emotional problems which may be associated with partially seeing children. To encourage the study of new ideas, practices, and techniques, and to disseminate this information among members of the group. To promote a closer social and professional relationship among teachers of the partially seeing."

CEPS Membership Requirements: Membership shall consist of professional and other persons who are members of CEC and are interested in the education of partially-seeing children and youth.

The Association of Homebound and Hospitalized Children (AEHHC) affiliated with CEC in April, 1958. Its purposes are:

". . . to promote a closer professional relationship among teachers of homebound and hospitalized children. To provide for the exchange of problems, new ideas, and solutions through the newsletter. To work for more extensive teacher training in the education of homebound and hospitalized children. To promote high professional standards. To provide for professional growth through workshops dealing with teaching the homebound and hospitalized in state, regional, and national meetings. To aid in teacher recruitment. To alert members to changes or proposed changes in legislation affecting homebound and hospitalized children."

AEHHC Membership Requirements: Membership is open to any CEC member actively engaged as a teacher, supervisor, or principal in the education of homebound and hospitalized children. Others interested in the education and welfare of these children are also welcome.

The Association for the Gifted (TAG) affiliated with CEC in April, 1958. Its purposes are:

". . . to promote the exchange of information concerning the gifted through regular regional and national meetings and through publications. To stimulate research. To work in ethically sound ways in the interest of the gifted. To inform people on what is known about the gifted and on current and new research in the area. To encourage people to become informed about the gifted."

TAG Membership Requirements: Membership is open to those members of CEC interested in the gifted.

The Council for Children with Behavioral Disorders (CCBD) affiliated with CEC in April, 1962. Its purposes are:

". . . to support the development of adequate services for children with behavioral disorders. To establish communication between local, state, and university programs for children with behavioral disorders. To promote adequate programs for teacher recruitment, training, and certification, and for educational research. To support favorable legislation."

CCBD Membership Requirements: Any member of CEC who is a professional worker in the field of the emotionally, socially, or neurologically handicapped, or is in a closely related field.

The Division on Mental Retardation (CEC-MR) affiliated with CEC in March, 1964. Its purposes are:

". . . to promote the education and general welfare of mentally retarded, research in the education of the retarded, the professional competency of personnel engaged in this field, and public understanding of the problems involved. To promote professional growth, research, and dissemination of research findings as a means of better understanding the problems related to the mentally retarded."

CEC-MR Membership Requirements: Any professional person directly concerned with the education of mentally retarded children, or who is in a field closely associated with it. All members shall be members of CEC.

The Division for Children with Communication Disorders (DCCD) affiliated with CEC in March, 1964. Its purposes are:

". . . to promote the education of children with communication disorders; to encourage and promote professional growth and research for the better understanding of the educational problems related to children with communication disorders."

DCCD Membership Requirements: Any person professionally engaged either in the education of children with communication disorders or in work directly related to their education. Members must hold membership in CEC.

There are many national groups which have had a significant effect on the development of programs for exceptional children. These organizations make their contributions in varying ways, but all have significant influence. Though there is always the risk of "offense by omission," the following list is given to illustrate the variety of organizations directly or indirectly involved with special education:

Alexander Graham Bell Association for the Deaf
The American Association on Mental Deficiency

American Association for Gifted Children
American Foundation for the Blind, Inc.
American Hearing Society
American Psychological Association
American Speech and Hearing Association
Association for the Aid of Crippled Children, Inc.
Muscular Dystrophy Association of America, Inc.
National Association for Retarded Children
The National Association for Gifted Children
National Association of Social Workers
National Society for the Prevention of Blindness
National Rehabilitation Association
National Multiple Sclerosis Society
National Epilepsy League, Inc.
National Society for Crippled Children and Adults
Speech Association of America
United Cerebral Palsy, Inc.
Volta Speech Association for the Deaf

These groups, and others, are available to help the special educator as he attempts to provide appropriate programs for exceptional girls and boys. The publications of these organizations provide a source of information which should not be overlooked, and the total effect of their efforts is more powerful than many would suppose.

LEGISLATION: WHAT TO DO ABOUT IT

It has been earlier inferred that legislation is quite important in developing or improving special education programs. This is a gross understatement. *Legislation is of the utmost importance* (good legislation, that is). The special educator must band together with others in his field as well as general educators to attempt to influence good legislation. Being heard is most important, but this task requires brainwork, plus a good set of vocal cords. The special educator must not overdo the emotional-appeal facet of education of the handicapped child, but he must not overlook its use when it is necessary to accomplish a strategic goal. Help from the various organizations (e.g., NARC, UCP) should be used carefully. The best method is to meet with these organizations on a nonpublicized basis, and plan a concerted attack from different vantage points. *Long range planning* is essential when doing legislative work. The whole matter takes time and effort, but the rewards may be considerable. The following areas are among those which may be influenced by proper legislation:

(a) Provision for better general reimbursement for special education programs

(b) Addition of new areas to be included as part of special education

(c) Better provision for cooperative districts

(d) Preschool programs for certain handicapping conditions

(e) A means to "mingle" school district funds with those of other agencies for joint operations

(f) Compulsory provision for ramps and elevators in *all* schools

(g) Legal authority for school districts to contract for certain services

(h) Provision for 100 per cent reimbursement for certain pilot programs

(i) Better state level consultative services

(j) Regulations which will encourage districts to send tuition students to adjoining districts for certain programs

(k) Provision of certain expensive individual-use equipment from the state level

(l) Reimbursement which makes expensive special education transportation less costly to the local district

(m) Compulsory laws relating to certain key programs

Obviously, states which already have good "legislative packages" in the area of special education may need little improvement, but with the accelerated "squeeze" on the tax dollar, these states should give most careful attention to maintaining their allotments.

HOW TO KEEP GOOD SPECIAL EDUCATION PERSONNEL

One major way to keep a good employee is to pay on a competitive basis. Since most teachers are on a salary schedule, this becomes the target for considerable effort. The special education administrator should encourage a starting wage schedule which pays enough to equal other school systems in the area; the salary should by all means reward length of service and advanced education. Certainly a type of merit pay might help, but since many teachers see this as a contentious word, perhaps it is better avoided. In addition, consider the following incentives:

(a) Provide for released time—during the day—for inservice work (this requires budgeting substitute teacher salaries).

(b) Establish short-term (two to four weeks) summer employment for master teachers to help develop and write new curriculum guides and teaching units.

(c) Provide time for attending various professional meetings.

(d) Bring in nationally known leaders in the field who can help lead the group toward new horizons.

(e) Always attempt to place new special classes in buildings where there is good administrative support for special education.

(f) Support good teachers and good teaching by getting rid of "dead wood."

(g) Arrange night and Saturday extension classes as the group expresses its needs or interests.

(h) *Really help* the staff with certification problems, materials, and equipment problems, and where possible, with personal problems.

(i) Do everything possible to make special education personnel feel "important" and "wanted." Listen to suggestions, attempt to rectify class grouping problems, and be alert for similar other trouble areas which are so important to the teacher.

PUBLIC RELATIONS AND SPECIAL EDUCATION

When planning public relations in relation to special education, there are at least four groups which must be considered. If an effective program of public relations is to be instituted, a different approach may be required for each group.

The largest group is that portion of the tax-paying public consisting of adults who do not have a son or daughter (or grandson or granddaughter) in a special education program. A second group is composed of parents of pupils who benefit from these programs. A third group consists of educators who know little about special education, except perhaps that such teachers receive a salary bonus for teaching the "small" but "special" class. A fourth group is the local board of education.

It should be immediately obvious that various facts and figures about special education must be presented differently to these various groups. State reimbursement, for example, is of greatest importance to the board of education. They must have the facts, when being harassed by local property tax owners about high per-pupil cost. They must also know something about the strengths of the program when being pressured by parent groups for more programs. State reimbursment data helps when dealing with "nonspecial education" parents, and in explaining any teacher salary differential to other educators. Also, when regular class teachers do not receive travel reimbursement for meeting attendance and special education personnel do (which is often the case), it is well for all involved to know that the state *requires* this meeting attendance for which separate state funds provide most of the travel cost.

That taking the educable mentally retarded pupil out of regular class is helpful to other pupils is of little value (public relations-wise) to parents of handicapped children, but may need to be used, in a tight spot, with other parents. Most sororities, fraternal groups, and service clubs can be appealed to when the total scope of special education is presented. It is often best to present a quick overview of all services, even if the major purpose of a formal presentation is to discuss one particular exceptionality.

Never be in the position of appearing to apologize for a program or lack of a program. Objectivity in admitting weaknesses is sound, but apologies or an apologetic manner is not in order.

The best public relations program a school system can buy is an excellent program of special education. Excellence sells with a minimum of planned public relations effort.

HOW TO IMPROVE YOUR PROGRAM

There are two important steps to improving your special education program. The first is self-appraisal. The second is initiating action to remedy shortcomings discovered by the self-appraisal. Sometimes it is wise to bring in an outside consultant to help you with the appraisal, and to suggest steps needed to remedy the problems discovered.

The outside expert may be better for two major reasons. The first is to lend objectivity to the appraisal. Sometimes we become so accustomed to walking around roadblocks, we no longer see the object blocking the road. A second value to utilizing an individual or team from outside your system is that recommendations made by "outside experts" may be more carefully considered than when made by local individuals.

The following questions might be used as a starting point for a quick self-appraisal:

How many exceptional children are living in your community? (Perhaps a revised method of surveying should be used.)

How is the school meeting the needs of these exceptional children? Are there different methods of meeting these needs? Have different methods really been given a try? Do you have an experimental program in the special education department? What things would you like to try, but have not because of money or lack of interest on the part of others? Could these be excuses? Could they be overcome with the proper approach?

Is your program a complete one, including both the elementary and secondary levels? Is the philosophy of teaching (for example, the mentally retarded) at the elementary and secondary school level the same?

How long has it been since you have had a good inservice training program which did something other than rehash the same old timeworn problems? Should you be doing more?

Have you attempted to work out special workshops with the nearest available teacher training institutions so that summer programs will really meet the needs of your teachers?

Is special education represented on the "superintendent's cabinet" meetings? If not, how could you bring about a change?

What has been the trend in the quality of teachers you have been able to employ in recent years? Do you get the same quality as the regular school program? If not, why not? Are you able to retain good teachers?

What does your school system do regarding assisting in place-ment of exceptional children after they have completed their pro-gram, or when they drop out? What more could be done? Do you have follow-up studies to determine the success or lack of success of these children? What curricular changes are needed to correct the factors which seem to cause lack of success?

After completing a self-appraisal (hopefully much more exten-sive than the one above), a plan to improve the existing program must be agreed upon. This should be outlined in sequential steps, with a target date established for each step. Unless the superin-tendent fully approves of the plan and intends to support it, it is of little use. Some changes may be instituted by the director alone, but almost always there are items relating to budget, building use, philosophy of education, administrator assignment, and other similar areas which absolutely require cooperative support at the top. Usually the superintendent will want to gain the support and endorsement of the board of education, or at least a commit-tee of the board, for any such plan.

The suggestions for improvement listed below might be of help in implementing change:

1. Visit and observe some of the school systems of comparable size in your state (and in other states) to see what they are doing in the area of special education.
2. Encourage teachers and supervisors to attend a variety of institutions of advanced learning to gain a variety of new ideas and approaches.
3. Make planned observational visits to the various colleges and universities having laboratory schools in special educa-tion.
4. Have representatives attend regional and national meetings which could serve to provide a source of new ideas, methods, and material.
5. Foster an atmosphere which encourages new thinking and discourages defensiveness with regard to existing ideas, methods, and philosophy.
6. Study legislative provisions which relate to special education and, if necessary, work with legislators to revise and im-prove laws and statutes.

7. Invite and encourage criticism and suggestions from school personnel outside the special education division of your school system.

Continued efforts to foster self-improvement are the key to maintaining a good program. If there is the will to do better, the knowledge that even good programs can be improved, plus a sincere belief that program improvement is one of the main functions of the special education administrator, efforts made on behalf of better implementation will always prove rewarding. If the goal is a more realistic learning experience for boys and girls, regularly organized attempts at high caliber programming are a "must."

XI

Program Development for the Mentally Retarded

By Edward Meyen[*]

INTRODUCTION

THE growth in special education services for the mentally retarded has been extensive in recent years. Enabling legislation and increased financial aid has enhanced this growth. However, in many communities, boards of education, yielding to the expressed concern of special interest groups, have embarked on the development of special education programs for the retarded, only to be finally content with the establishment of a single special class.

The development of a special education program for the mentally retarded requires more than administrative decisions and grouping of children. It requires a commitment on the part of educators and lay boards to structure a sequential program of educational experience from preschool through the secondary level. Many administrators fail to recognize that once a child is placed in a special class, the class activities tend to become the educational program for this particular child. While the child may participate in extracurricular activities with his normal peers and at times attend selected regular classes, rarely will he return to the regular stream of the school program. Cognizant of this, ad-

---

[*] Mr. Meyen's experience is both extensive and varied. His classroom experience includes teaching the educable mentally retarded at the junior high level in the public schools, and serving as a demonstration teacher in the Special Education Laboratory School at Colorado State College. From 1960 to 1964 he was Consultant for the Mentally Retarded with the Iowa State Department of Public Instruction. He later served as director of Iowa's project to develop a "Comprehensive Plan to Combat Mental Retardation." Mr. Meyen is currently an instructor at the University of Iowa where he is a doctoral candidate.

115

ministrators must seek to develop special education programs capable of providing a total educational program for retarded children and youth. This means the program must have both scope and sequence.

In the early years of special education for the mentally retarded, a single class was often initiated at the age level commensurate with the largest group of retarded children in the system. This frequently was at the intermediate level for children from ten to fourteen years of age. If the number of eligible pupils was insufficient to fill a class, students with borderline ability or with behavioral problems were often placed there to warrant establishment of the class. The typical special class in many districts was characterized by a wide age range, inadequate facilities and was taught by a marginally-trained teacher with little direction from the administrator. Today the pitfalls of such an approach are apparent; the emphasis is now on the development of comprehensive programs aimed at preparing the retarded child for a productive life.

While attention was being given to classes for the mentally retarded, special education for exceptional children in general was gaining in status as an integral part of our educational system. This status has been attained despite the connotation of the term "special" and its application to special classes, special services, and special equipment. The utilization of this term has tended to accentuate the differences between learning experiences for the exceptional child and those of the "normal" child. At the same time, use of this term has resulted in some administrators viewing special classes and services as apart from the general program, thus failing to consider special education needs when planning curriculum revisions, inservice education and building programs.

Unlike children with remedial problems which can be corrected, the mentally retarded need a total educational program geared to their slow rate of development. Special help and tutoring, while helpful, will not be sufficient. Educators have explored varying curriculum modifications in an attempt to effectively meet the needs of the retarded, and at the same time facilitate the learning experiences of the "normal" child. The special class with a small enrollment taught by a teacher with additional preparation has become the pattern for educational programming for the retarded.

Today, most school districts are providing some educational experiences for retarded children. A smaller but significant number are offering extended programs through the secondary level; however, there has been no set pattern to their development. Some were planned and implemented in phases; others have evolved from a single class to several on different levels, but with little continuity. Thus, it would be presumptuous to suggest a step-by-step approach to the development of a comprehensive special education program for the mentally retarded. On the other hand, there is no common point in an approach to developing programs which would be applicable to the status of special education in most districts. With this in mind, consideration will be given to total programming, and suggestions will be offered on all levels of operation. If the administrator of a district is offering special classes on a limited scale, he will find a rationale for expansion of his program. The administrator of a district with a program of considerable scope will find this chapter will aid him in the evaluation of his operation. Administrators embarking on a new program will find a frame of reference as to what constitutes an adequate program, and suggestions applicable to the different stages of program development.

This chapter will focus on the essential components to total programming for the mentally retarded. In general, it will be assumed that the district is of sufficient size and possesses the necessary resources required to develop and maintain a comprehensive educational program for the retarded. Modifications in programming which can be applied to this proposed framework of services for school districts faced with limited resources or a small population, will also be discussed. While such factors may greatly restrict the provision of special education services to the mentally retarded within individual districts, they need not preclude the availability of such services. Instructional programs for the trainable mentally retarded will be discussed separately from special education programs for the educable.

IDENTIFICATION

When facing the problem of identifying educable mentally retarded children in a given school system, there is often a tendency to consider only those pupils presenting the obvious problems in the regular classes. It is assumed that those who do not pose significant problems for the teacher are evidently progressing satisfactorily. They may be attending classes and not causing management or instructional problems; but the questions are: Are they gaining what they should? Would keeping them in the regular class be the most effective educational approach for these particular children? Also to be considered is the added burden to the regular classroom teacher.

It must be recognized that the larger the number of retarded children available for programming, the greater the opportunities for effective grouping. Because of this, there is also the danger of attempting to maximize the number of children eligible for special class placement by compromising on the admission policies, e.g., by considering children with IQ's in the low 80's to increase the number of candidates for a given class. The same applies when placement in a special class for the mentally retarded is used for children functioning below capacity because of behavioral problems. Fortunately, such practices are inhibited by the enactment of legislation and/or approval policies by state boards of education.

In contrast to the trainable mentally retarded, the educable present few physical clues to their identity. Most appear like any other boy or girl their age. They are rarely identified until faced with a situation in which they cannot respond appropriately because of their social and/or intellectual limitations. While they are academically slow in their performance in class, there may be other children achieving at the same level who are academically but not mentally retarded. Differentiating between the educational needs of the retarded and pupils with other learning difficulties is essential if the specific needs of children are to be met.

Prior to undertaking identification activities, the administrator should acquaint himself with the approval policies of the state's department of publc instruction. Many such departments offer consultants to assist in preliminary planning. These persons have the advantage of having worked with a variety of districts in the development of programs, thus are sensitive to the pitfalls of establishing a program, as well as to the unique public relation problems which may exist. To facilitate the benefits gained from consultative services from these departments, it is advisable to confer with the administrative staff and selected teachers so that questions and problems posed to the consultants are well-formulated and relevant to the task of establishing a program. The screening process and organizational tasks necessary for initiating classes may require six months to a year, thus, involvment of the state agency should occur in the early stages of planning the activities.

Two conditions are basic to the initial decision-making on the part of the superintendent. He must recognize that provisions can be made to enhance educational programs for the educable mentally retarded; he also must be sensitive to the views of the regular teachers, building principals, and special service personnel whose experience suggests that there are children in the district requiring special education. Once these conditions are met, the task of identification must be faced. Many children, by virtue of their performance in regular classes, will be generally known to their principals and teachers. This also applies to the siblings of families whose children have repeatedly experienced failure in school. Others will be known as contributors to discipline problems in the classroom and, therefore, would be suspect as mentally retarded. On the other hand, there will be a large number of children within the educable range in need of special class placement whose identity will be less obvious because their pattern of behavior is cooperative and less demanding. Their teachers accept them as slow and feel no pressure to make them perform. Still others will be shielded because of the status their family has attained in the community. These factors combine to complicate the identification process.

Approaches to the Identification Process

Referral Approach

Inservice training sessions can be held, during which time emphasis should be given to the need for special education classes for the educable mentally retarded. The administration's interest in programming for this population of children should also be expressed. Teachers should then be provided with information to assist in their understanding of the mentally retarded and to improve their skills in identifying them. As a result of the inservice training, reliance on referral to the psychologist might be necessary as the initial manner of identifying the retarded. *The time required and the possibilities of over- and/or under-referral generally preclude extensive use of this procedure in the initial development of programs.* However, once operational, this approach can be developed as a sound referral source.

Screening Approach

This method systematically attempts to identify all children in need of special class placement. Although a variety of procedures may be used, the following guidelines should be considered:

1. The system should be efficient in that the number of over-referrals to the psychologist for psychological evaluation should be minimal. Both teacher judgment and objective test results should be employed.
2. Manpower demands should be kept in balance. If the number of children to be evaluated is too great for the psychological services staff, the result may be a compromise in the quality of the evaluation. One alternative is to limit the screening for a new program to kindergarten through the sixth or ninth grades. Later, as the program is expanded, screening can be extended to the upper grades.

When undertaking a screening program to identify mentally retarded children, the objective is to be as efficient as possible in identifying those children in need of special class placement; however, the number of children who are functioning below expectations, but are not mentally retarded and are being seen by the psychologist, should be minimized. Obviously, this latter group of children requires curriculum modification. But in establishing a new class or classes, the time required for individual psychological examination precludes administering it as a general screening device to all children. Thus, considerable effort in planning should be exerted to reduce the number of overreferrals to the school psychologist.

A screening procedure used in many districts consists of the following:

1. Asking the teachers to rank their students according to ability in reading and arithmetic from the most competent to the least competent.
2. Following the teacher appraisal, the most recent achievement test scores for the same academic areas are recorded. In addition, results of group intelligence tests are used as a third variable. Should group IQ test data not be available, such tests can be administered by the classroom teacher under the direction of the school psychologist or guidance counselor.

On the basis of these variables, namely, teacher judgment, achievement level, and group intelligence test scores, the lower 25 per cent of the children per grade level should be reviewed through a staffing involving the classroom teacher, building principal, and school psychologist. The objective of the conference should be to determine which students appear most likely to be within the educable range. These children should then be referred for an individual psychological examination.

Suggested Guidelines

No reference should be made to selecting pupils for special class placement in conferring with regular classroom teachers regarding the appraisal of their pupils' skills in reading and arithmetic. Instead, emphasis should be placed on pupils with learning problems. Many teachers view mental retardation solely in terms of family background and may be inclined to underrate some of the children because of this presumption; whereas if the achievement level is stressed, there may be less consideration of the social implications.

The teacher appraisal should be recorded on a form separate from that used for recording the achievement and group intelligence test data, in order to discourage the teachers from referring to the cumulative records.

It is also advisable to require the appraisals to be done during a specified period of time. Teachers should be assured that this is not an attempt to evaluate their instructing abilities, but merely one of several steps in the identification of children with learning problems.

A conference with the teacher, building principal and psychologist should be held to review the status of the children in the lower 25 per cent range, once the instructor appraisals, achievement test scores and group intelligence data are available and recorded. Particular attention should be given to the chronological age, years retained, and cases of prolonged absence from school. Those children for whom the available data suggests low ability and comparable performance should be referred to the psychologist for individual psychological examination.

A case study of the social, developmental, and family history of each candidate should be conducted and made available to the psychologist prior to the psychological examination.

Scheduling pupils for psychological examination requires considerable planning since a psychologist generally can evaluate (approximately) only four children per day. It should be noted that normally the routine testing done by school psychologists will not be limited to the mentally retarded; however, in the screening process for a new program, in order to accomplish the task, it will be necessary to focus the psychological services on this specific assignment. Later, as the program becomes operational and expands, the demand for psychological services will level off, and candidates for special classes can be seen on a referral basis. It may be advisable to obtain additional psychological services from adjoining districts, intermediate school district, private sources, or the state's department of public instruction to facilitate the final evaluations. In states which require parent approval prior to psychological evaluation, this rule must, of course, be followed.

Data collected through the screening process should be entered in the student's cumulative folder. Some districts find it necessary to design a separate insert to record data relative to special class placement.

Children recommended for placement by the psychologist should be referred to their family physician for a complete physical examination as part of the final screening process. If the school employs a physician, the examination may be conducted through the health service. It is important to identify any physical problems which may be contributing to the child's learning problem. It is not uncommon to find children with correctable vision, hearing, or general health problems which are not identified through routine health checks in the classroom.

Child Study Committee

A committee should be established whose function will be to consider the results of various screening procedures and to make final recommendations relative to placement. The participation of committee members will be dependent on their involvement in the cases being considered. Representatives may include the following:

1. School Psychologists
2. School Nurse
3. Building Principal
4. Special Education Director
5. Regular Classroom Teacher
6. Special Education Teacher

In some districts the child study committee considers the placement for all special education programs; the membership is modified depending upon the child to be seen and the program being considered for the particular child. If this is the case, the director of special education may be designated as the chairman of the child study committee to coordinate the preliminary case information activities. Using the structure of a child study committee to make decisions on placement provides greater assurance that the child will receive the benefit of a total comprehensive examination; also, that the decision for placement will not be on the basis of a single examination or the perspective of one discipline. The same committee structure might be used during the operations of the program for re-evaluation of children being considered for transfer to other classes or for return to a regular class.

PLACEMENT DECISION

1. Special class placement should initially be on a trial basis for a short period of time to allow the individual adequate opportunity for adjustment. This is particularly important if there is some resistance on the part of the parents to the child's placement in the special class. The trial placement gives the child a chance to adjust. As the child adjusts to the new learning situation, there is an opportunity for the parents to develop a better understanding of the child's limitations and abilities.

2. During the trial period the special education teacher should keep an extensive anecdotal record which should reflect the progress or lack of progress made by the individual during this period.

3. The supervisor, director, and/or psychologist should visit the class at regular intervals and observe the child participating in learning experiences. This is particularly important during the early stages of a new class, since the children will be coming from different classes; the teacher may need guidance and assistance in organizing her group and orienting the pupils to the new program.

4. If the behavior, social development, and/or progress of an individual indicates the need for exclusion from the program or a change of program, the parents should be made aware of the contributing factors prior to the time of the decision.

Communicating with Parents

Frequently, parents of educable mentally retarded children are reluctant to consent to special class placement. Some of the reluctance is justified, however; in many cases the hesitancy is a result of inadequate communication on the part of school officials.

A large per cent of the educable mentally retarded population comes from families of low economic means. It is not uncommon to find several siblings in one family functioning within educable or borderline levels. Often, one or both of the parents are intellectually limited. Because of these environmental conditions and the general intellectual limitations of the family members, the previous school relations may have been less than desirable. This does not imply that the family does not value an education for the child; it does imply that the history of school failure and frequent conferences related to educational problems have caused many such families to view the school with suspicion. Any educational treatment of their child different from the regular program arouses their concern. This is particularly true when they are informed of the decision of special class placement without previous preparation. Their first reaction is often one of rejection, thinking that the school is attempting to group their child with others in an instructional program convenient to the administration. Because of this, administrators must be cautious in their approach. The following suggestions should be considered:

Reporting procedures in regular classes provide the basis for parent conferences relative to a child's placement in a special class. If the regular teacher has been cognizant of the child's learning problems and honest in his reporting to the parents, the confrontation with the school's interest in improving the child's instructional program through special class placement will not be a surprise. However, if the teacher has generously reported satisfactory or borderline progress which has been interpreted by the parents as reasonable for their child, then one can expect a negative reaction to the idea of special class placement. In many situations, because of lenient reporting in the primary grades, parents are not aware of the significance of their child's intellectual limitations; they feel that the school's decision for special class placement is unfair and unjustified.

There is sufficient time to prepare parents for the possibility of their child needing special education because the screening process and organizational aspects of developing special classes is time-consuming. Once a child has been referred for a psychological evaluation, the parents should be invited to the school for a conference with the regular teacher. During this time they should be introduced to the school psychologist, who informs them that the school is interested in helping their child progress better in his school performance, and that more information is needed regarding his strengths and weaknesses. The matter of administering additional tests can be discussed. In this way the ground work is established relative to later discussions following future test results, and permission for testing can be obtained.

Parents should be encouraged to observe the child in school activities. The teacher should be prepared to illustrate the child's learning problems (during conferences) by comparing his work with that normally expected of children in his particular grade or age level.

Should the test results indicate special class placement and the child study committee's recommendation be in favor of placing the child in the special class, an additional parent conference should be held. If possible, there may be some advantage to holding this conference in the family home. The psychologist should be involved in the conference and be given responsibility for interpreting the test results to the parents. It may be advantageous to include a second person who has established a good relationship with the family, for example, the school nurse, social worker, visiting teacher, or possibly a regular teacher who previously taught one of the siblings in class. During the conference, the school representatives should emphasize such positive aspects of the special class as small pupil-teacher ratio, individualized instruction and opportunities for future experiences which will offer the child vocational success. Questions pertaining to future programs for the child should he be placed in the class, represent an area in which the school may be somewhat vulnerable in terms of establishing a new program. That is, if the district is just embarking on a special class program, chances are the program will be initiated at the elementary level, while the secondary or high school program may not even be in existence. With this in mind, school representatives must be in a position to indicate to the parents the plans of the school district relative to providing additional classes. Emphasis should be given to the long-range development of a program which will have scope and sequence, with appropriate vocational opportunities available to the youth as he progresses through the program.

If the parents are very negative toward special class placement, involving the special class teacher in the initial conference must be avoided. The special class teacher will thus not be identified with this initial concern on the part of the parents. He will later have an opportunity to develop his own relationship with the family, which will place him at considerable advantage in working with the child.

Strive for consent on the part of the parents for placement of their child in the special class. In many states, the board of education has the legal authority to determine placement of a child in the particular program which best meets the educational needs of the child. Placement against the wishes of the parents should be made only as a last resort. The initial placement in this case should be considered a trial placement, with special emphasis given to demonstrating during this period that the program is appropriate for the child.

Do not send a letter as the first means of informing the parents that their child should report to a special class next fall. First, it is extremely difficult to structure a letter which conveys the intended meaning; and secondly, it can later become a source of poor public relations should the parents choose publicly to contest the placement.

SPECIAL CLASS FACILITIES

Although the establishment of a climate conducive to programming for the mentally retarded and the legislating of financial subsidy to local districts have received considerable attention the planning of physical facilities in which the learning experiences take place have been grossly ignored. This is in contrast to the progress made by education in the preparation of special class teachers. Many special classes came into being during an era in which school districts were being reorganized and classroom space was at a premium. As a result, except for building programs which have since been initiated, there was little opportunity to plan facilities giving adequate consideration to educational programs for the mentally retarded. Consequently, administrators were immediately faced with decisions regarding housing for special classes. Many classes were relegated to a residential house down the street, to the basement of the First Baptist Church, or even to the twice-condemned, but neat and clean rural school house at the edge of town. While many classes have survived in spite of these conditions, and good teaching practices have prevailed, a greater number have experienced considerable difficulty or have developed an undesirable status as a result of these housing practices.

For those faced with problems of space limitations, but who are interested in initiating special classes for the mentally retarded, the following guidelines should be considered in reaching important decisions.

CLASSROOM FACTORS

Quality

The quality of the facility is often interpreted by the public as indicating the general acceptance of the class by the administration as an integral part of the total school program. Special classes held in regular elementary attendance centers with little attempt to identify the special class as anything other than another elementary class, have a much better chance of maintaining their identity in the total school program than those operated in separate facilities. An equally important factor is that church basements, residential homes and other structures are not designed for classroom activities; use of these places can result in frequent compromises in the instructional program.

Integration/Segregation

If facilities other than the regular school plant must be utilized for classes, this does not necessarily mean that the logical class to be held in the separate facilities should be the special class. As mentioned earlier in this chapter, special education classes for the educable mentally retarded constitute the *educational* program for retarded children, just as the regular classes and extra-curricular activities constitute the educational program for "normal" children. While a child will spend one year in the second grade, then progress to the third and following grades, the retarded child may be three to four years in the same special class, then may progress through three or four such levels of special classes throughout his entire educational program. Should a choice exist when separate facilities must be used, placement in a regular rather than a special class might yield the least negative consequences in the long run. This suggestion is offered in view of the social advantages to the child, as well as the advantages accrued by the special class teacher in becoming a participating member of the faculty.

Coupled with these advantages is the argument that parents will be more inclined to accept the program in the regular elementary attendance center. This is particularly true of new classes. From the parents' point of view, when Johnny walks in the front door of Smith Elementary School, he is "going to school"; however, when he enters a school for the retarded, whether it is in a church basement or the house down the street, parents and the public in general are conscious he is going to the "special" school. This may sound as if unwarranted concessions should be made to the retarded. This is not the case; rather, it is an attempt to enhance the learning experiences of the children placed in special classes, while at the same time alleviating other administrative problems. It is not suggested that special classes for the mentally retarded should be housed only in the best facilities in the district; but they *should* be on a par with those facilities used for the regular grades. Once a special class program is developed and accepted by staff and community, then there may be situations when separate facilities could be utilized without detrimental affect.

Chronological Placement

Special classes for retarded children should be located adjacent to classes for "normal" children of similar chronological age. While many districts comply with this suggestion, a number also group special classes within an attendance center. There are advantages in this arrangement for the special class teacher; it affords her a more effective means of communication, plus an opportunity to exchange materials and equipment with other special class teachers. However, if the attendance center is large, much can be gained on the part of the regular students if the classes are placed strategically throughout the building. This results in the special class being less conspicuous; interaction between the special and regular pupils is also facilitated.

Family-Living Unit

In terms of structural characteristics of special classrooms, the educational specifications are basically the same as for regular classes. Although the pupil-teacher ratio may be approximately one-half of that of the regular classes, the classroom activities require the same square footage as recommended for regular classes serving children of camparable ages. The basic difference at the elementary level centers around the demands of the curriculum for a self-contained unit. Emphasis on family living, social development and practical arts makes the inclusion of a kitchen or family unit station within the classroom an important consideration. Such a unit might include a sink, cupboards, stove, refrigerator and ample storage. Because of frequent group activity, the furniture should be movable. The wide age range in many special classes dictates the need for adjustable furniture. Since many of the materials used in the class will be teacher-made, a work area for the teacher is definitely desirable.

Many programs housing a number of classes for the educable mentally retarded in a single attendance center find a family-living unit extremely helpful for providing training experiences. Such a unit is often comprised of a kitchen, bedroom, living room and bathroom. Since this space is expensive, the rooms need not be large. Also, cost is reduced through maximum utilization of the facilities. If located in a junior or senior high school facility, it can serve the home economic needs of the regular program. If incorporated in an elementary plant, the unit can be located adjacent to facilities used for faculty meetings and community activities; it could always be available for regular classroom use. Again, the costs are more than justified if the unit is planned for maximum use.

Junior-Senior High School Unit

On the junior and senior high school levels the requirements for physical facilities are determined by the organization of the program. In a core-type program in which special class teachers teach a specific area such as practical math, social studies, or communication skills, with students rotating between the classes, then the structural requirements are basically similar to those for regular classes. This, of course, assumes that industrial arts and home economics facilities are available to the special class students for experiences in the practical arts. The same would apply to the work-study programs as discussed later. However, if the program is to be self-contained (as is the situation in many small districts where only one or two classes are operated at the junior and/or senior high levels) then the classroom must be designed to accommodate the full range of curriculum experiences. This means that in addition to the necessary space for general academic type experiences, facilities for home economics and industrial arts activities must be provided.

Even if the full range of regular educational facilities is available for the special class, access to a living unit as previously discussed will greatly facilitate the providing of meaningful experiences. In addition to the social benefits resulting from use of the living unit, considerable vocational-type experiences can be developed at the junior-senior high levels through this unit.

The School Principal

The competence and cooperation of the building principal are vital; if the classes are to succeed, the teacher(s) will need considerable support from the principal. While supervisory services may be available from a central consultant staff, the special class teacher should maintain the same relationship with the building principal as do the regular classroom teachers. The principal must understand the educational needs of the retarded child, and also be sensitive to the administrative demands or decisions which may result from having a special class in his building.

Unfortunately, many principals claim a lack of knowledge of special education, so will concede to the teacher or special education director many decisions which by all rights should be made by the principal. Through inservice education and professional reading, the principal can strengthen his skills and increase his knowledge of special education. It should be noted that in general the pupils placed in special classes for the educable mentally retarded are the ones previously served in regular classes, so children at this functioning level are not new to the principal. The separate classes, employment of curriculum modification, and labeling of the program represent the only changes. These same factors are present when educational innovations in terms of grouping and new instructional programs are introduced in the regular program. Thus, experienced principals should have competence and skills applicable to the administration of school programs, including special education classes for the mentally retarded.

Traffic Patterns

In establishing a new special class in an existing elementary school, the administration may be restricted in the modifications of the classroom; however, certain arrangements can be made. When new building programs are anticipated, consideration should be given to the traffic flow and the relationship of the special class to other rooms and facilities. Although the self-contained classroom is typical of most programs at the elementary level, a certain amount of movement is made by all students. For example, in utilizing the lunchroom, restrooms, multi-purpose rooms, and physical education facilities, children are required to leave the classroom.

No unique or significant health problems can be generalized with the educable mentally retarded. However, because of the deprived situations from which many of these youngsters come, the incidence of general health problems may be higher among this group. Thus, consideration might be given to the accessibility of the nurse's office.

For most educable children no problems will be encountered in using the regular restroom facilities. However, for younger primary-age educable mentally retarded children and preschoolers, training in personal hygiene may receive a major amount of emphasis in the curriculum, so the inclusion of restroom facilities in the classroom may be advantageous. For the older children, use of public facilities is part of the training in developing independence. Normal precautions should be exercised to accommodate those youngsters with special physical problems.

Because mentally retarded children are limited in making judgements and spontaneous decisions, accessibility to outside exits must be considered in the interest of emergencies. Educable youngsters may effectively participate in routine emergency drills; however, they cannot be expected to carry out detailed instructions during a time of stress.

TRANSPORTATION

The prevalence of children within the educable mentally retarded range will vary. Generally, administrators can expect to find approximately 2 to 3 per cent of the school age population within this level of functioning. In some areas, the impact of deprived social and economic conditions may yield a higher proportion of children in the educable range. While this 2 to 3 per cent of the school population may seem large when applied to the average daily attendance of the district, it may be quite small when applied to a particular attendance center. Organizing special classes to group children with a minimum of individual differences, and at the same time to house the classes in schools with children of comparable age may be difficult. For example, in an elementary school serving four hundred children there may be eight educable mentally retarded children with a range in age from five to twelve years, and a range in I.Q. from 50 to 80. In the development of an instructional program on different levels with only eight children, many compromises would be required unless the population base could be increased. This frequently is accomplished by transporting children from several centers to one location. When the population base is increased to assure the availability of enough mentally retarded children for grouping, then the problem of transportation often arises. Educable mentally retarded children can ride the regular school bus with other children with a minimum of difficulty. However, transporting pupils between attendance centers is not easily accommodated without modifications in the routing of buses.

Alternatives in Transportation

1. Have pupils ride regular buses or walk to the attendance center they normally would attend; then use a shuttle bus to transport these pupils to the school providing the special class.
2. Utilize public transportation services. With the exception of the primary age pupil, most educable mentally retarded children at the elementary level (with instruction) can ride a public bus.
3. Contract with a private person or firm to operate a special bus service.
4. Contract with parents to transport children to special classes. Because of potential liability problems and the excessive cost of operating numerous small transportation programs, this alternative is considered less than desirable.

Most states include in their state aid program provision for additional subsidy to districts transporting handicapped pupils. When transportation is required, attention should be given to establishing a schedule that exerts a minimum of influence on the curriculum, i.e., avoid starting class 20 minutes late and dismissing 30 minutes early to comply with the established bus schedule.

REPORTING PUPIL PROGRESS

The major purpose of report cards and parent-teacher conferences is to inform parents of the progress their child is making in his educational program. However, there is an additional dimension to these practices which is often overlooked, but which is of particular significance in terms of special education for the mentally retarded. The information conveyed to parents through report cards and/or parent-teacher conferences tends to reflect the philosophy and general content of the educational experiences afforded the children attending the particular school. For example, a typical report card for a regular junior high school would probably include a listing of specific subjects such as science, mathematics, language arts, social studies and possibly a foreign language. A review of such report cards gives some indication of the nature of the program and the relative emphasis given to the different subjects. The academic orientation is apparent. In essence, report cards communicate both the child's performance and the nature of his program. This should be true when reporting the progress of a child in the special class. In other words, the report should give some indication of the curriculum implemented in the special class.

Because the curriculum differs for the child in the special class, the criteria for reporting pupil progress should also differ. Areas in which grades are reported should correlate with areas stressed in the curriculum. Assuming that the teacher is stressing social adjustment and a practical approach to the teaching of skill subjects, the report should reflect the respective orientation of the curriculum. This, of course, means the design of a report card specific to the special education program. Although the development of a separate card will necessitate considerable involvement on the part of the special class teacher, the time will be well spent. A well-designed report card commensurate with the instructional program can be a meaningful tool in helping parents recognize what is educationally significant for their child. This applies at all age levels. If the program is structured properly, and pupil progress is systematically reported accordingly, the parents are frequently reminded of what the school considers realistic for their child. This does not mean, necessarily, that the parents will immediately change their attitudes if they previously have been sensitive regarding their child's placement in a special class.

Some districts prefer not to use report cards. Instead, parent-teacher conferences are utilized. There are advantages to parent conferences in that the teacher gains feedback and can check on the parent's understanding of the child's functioning level. The same suggestions relative to reflecting the orientation of the curriculum through the use of report cards apply to parent-teacher conferences. There are potential problems inherent in the routine use of conferences relative to parents of mentally retarded children. These are cited not to discourage their use but, rather, to alert administrators so that the problems can be avoided.

Because the presence of a mentally retarded child has considerable impact on a family, parents frequently have need for counseling, or at least direction in how to facilitate their child's development. Often the school is the only resource for such assistance in the community. The school psychologist, teacher, and/or principal may offer some reinforcement, or arrange for referral to specialized services such as the mental health clinic or to private sources. However, school personnel in general are not trained to counsel parents experiencing severe emotional problems relative to their child's retardation.

Teachers should recognize their own limitations and approach conferences with the basic objective of providing parents with information relevant to their child's educational program and overall development. The teacher, in disseminating such information, should be supportive, but at the same time sensitive to the parent's reaction and expressed concerns. The dangers of the teacher's becoming too involved with parents in a counseling situation are numerous. For example, the parents may identify with the teacher and continue to seek her counsel while postponing professional counseling services. She is vulnerable in that the parents soon begin to pose questions in areas beyond her competence and/or jurisdiction. The teacher may feel compelled to venture an answer or to express an opinion which is later interpreted as fact. There is always the possibility that a conflict may develop. When this happens, the teacher's relationship with her pupils is endangered by parental attitudes. Parent-teacher conferences should focus on the child's educational and developmental status. Teacher-parent relationships of a counseling nature should be minimized.

Regardless of the procedure established for reporting pupil progress to parents, some basic considerations apply, namely:

1. Because of the importance given to grades in the public schools, parents and children alike have certain expectations of reporting procedures. These expectations are conditioned by the prevailing practices in the regular program. This is particularly important at the junior and senior high levels where peer pressure for grades and certain kinds of report cards is considerable. Consideration should be given to complying with practices established throughout the system. For example, while the content in a report card may vary, its general appearance, structure, and dissemination schedule should be as similar as possible to those in the regular program. Conferences should be scheduled according to the pattern of the system; supplemental conferences might also be periodically held.

2. The criteria for reporting progress should reflect the curriculum and be geared to the child's performance. The latter is problematic because norms are not available. Progress should be measured in terms of the pupil's performance relative to his current potential. Emphasis should be on the child's functioning level.

3. Use of letter grades should be avoided; however, if they are to be used, their meaning should be well explained, since, in special classes, they can frequently result in misunderstanding. Parents usually think of *A, B, C,* as implying certain levels of performance. To them an *A* is an *A* regardless of who earned the grade. It is very difficult to establish a double standard for letter grades. However, if reasonable understanding can be developed and the grades appropriately documented in the pupil's cumulative record, they may serve the purpose sufficiently.

INSERVICE TRAINING

The contrast between the demand for special class teachers and the supply provided by colleges and universities has been significant in recent years. There is reason to believe that the gap between supply and demand will widen in years to come.

Research on the effectiveness of early education of retarded children is stimulating public schools to program at the preschool level and to initiate early placement; districts having provided special classes only at the elementary level in the past are establishing secondary classes and work-study programs; reorganization of school districts, heretofore too small to make special class grouping feasible, are now being combined into larger units; and the implementation of Title I of Pl-89-10 is resulting in varying modifications of programs for mentally retarded and educationally disadvantaged youth. While the emphasis of these new and/or extended programs is somewhat diverse, there is a common element in that their successful implementation is dependent upon the procurement of teachers with the same general training and personal characteristics as those of good special class teachers for the mentally retarded.

The nation-wide growth of special classes has been rapid. However, concomitant with this growth in classes for the educable mentally retarded is the problem of assuring continuity in the scope of the curriculum. Because of teacher shortages, administrators must frequently compromise in the employment of teachers with less than the desired training and experience. Special education directors, principals, and general curriculum coordinators (while competent in their administrative and coordinative roles) rarely possess the background and/or time to assist effectively the special class teacher in methodology and preparation of instructional materials. These factors, coupled with the varying approaches to educating mentally retarded children promulgated by teacher-training institutions, place the special class teacher in a somewhat unusual position. Ideas on methodology, materials, and modifications, which combine to constitute what inservice training she may receive, must be gleaned from the literature and from her colleagues in the regular and special class. Or, her inservice training needs are met through arbitrarily being assigned to subject matter sections of inservice training programs designed for regular classroom teachers. It must, of course, be acknowledged that special class teachers can benefit from this; however, they should be allowed to exercise some selection in the areas in which they participate.

A major deterrent to the development of inservice training programs for special class teachers has been the lack of sufficient numbers of teachers in a given school district to warrant the expenditure of funds and the organizational task involved. This is not to imply a value judgment on the needs of special class teachers for inservice training, but to accent a practical consideration in planning inservice education for a total faculty. In most situations, cooperation with adjoining districts is necessary to obtain an adequate number of teachers. While there will be certain goals that the administration may wish to accomplish through inservice training, a significant portion of such training experiences should result from the expressed needs of the teachers. Programs should be planned which involve teacher participation. Consultants can be used when appropriate, but they should be carefully selected; nothing is more deadly than a two-hour lecture by an uninspiring speaker on an irrelevant topic. If the topic warrants the employment of an outside consultant, it merits the selection of a capable specialist. The talent of local special class teachers, directors of special education, principals and other faculty members should not be overlooked.

A project often used with special class teachers as a form of inservice training is the development of a curriculum guide. This has merit and can yield considerable return to the teacher, pupils, and school program in general. However, it is not the best "first" inservice training activity to be undertaken. The development of a curriculum guide requires leadership, skill, knowledge, and perseverance. Although these attributes may be possessed singly or otherwise by different teachers on the staff, until they have worked together and gained experience with their children, it will be difficult to determine which persons possess which strengths. Many such projects bog down because the teachers are not prepared to make the required decisions, nor do they feel competent in pursuing a venture of such scope. It is wiser to begin with projects aimed at short-term goals and geared to the needs of the teachers. As they gain experience and begin to view inservice training as beneficial to them, they will develop in leadership, as well as the other attributes required for more extensive projects. It is particularly important that these training programs, once initiated, continue in a sequential pattern. The sessions should be scheduled and topics announced well in advance so that the teachers can anticipate the experience and be prepared to participate. It should also be mentioned that the programs should be geared for teachers at different levels. Secondary teachers naturally will have needs different from those of elementary teachers.

While teacher-training programs at college and university level must be strengthened and expanded to meet the growing needs for special class teachers, the inroad to improvement of instructional practices in the classroom for a number of years to come must be through special class teachers presently in the field. Extension courses are an alternative, but as a vehicle to cope with this situation, they have limitations. Basically, they introduce the factors of grades, transfer of credit, prescribed course content, and the problem of accessibility to all teachers. Inservice training is a logical approach, but the program must be planned and systematic; the topics considered must be commensurate with the needs of the teacher.

Inservice Training Suggestions

1. If there is a small number of special class teachers in the school system (e.g., 4-5), administrators should cooperate with adjoining districts in developing an inservice training program.
2. Topics should be selected according to the expressed concern of the teachers involved.
3. Early projects should have short-term goals which require active involvement on the part of the teachers.
4. If the special class teachers also are to be given an opportunity to participate in the inservice training program for regular teachers, they should have enough advance information on the topic to make a decision on the relevance of the topic to their program.
5. Although attention should be given to selecting topics and projects appropriate to different ability levels, additional activities should be planned which require the participation of teachers from all levels of the special-class program.

6. Use the inservice training sessions to facilitate communication between teachers and special-service personnel.
7. Since the teacher's participation in an inservice program should help improve the instructional program, release time is warranted for some of the sessions. However, in many cases sessions one to two hours in length after school will be sufficient.
8. A schedule should be established for all sessions and changes should be kept at a minimum.
9. Sessions should be brief, but meaningful; assignments could be made during the interim between sessions.

CURRICULUM

The justification for special classes is often credited to the ineffectiveness of the regular class system in educating the mentally retarded. This rationale is based on the premise that the academic orientation which typifies the curriculum in general education is not appropriate to the educational needs of the mentally retarded. Those who support this view feel that educational outcomes for the mentally retarded must be more than academic achievement in basic skills. They acknowledge that the curriculum should emphasize the practical application of basic skills; however, they also stress that considerable emphasis should be given to social development, improvement of self-concept, and adaptability.

While there tends to be general agreement on this philosophy, considerable variance is reflected in the instructional programs implemented in special classes. Teachers vary in terms of how they perceive the curriculum for the educable mentally retarded. In general, they agree philosophically that the program should be practical, have high utility value and be geared to the functioning level of the child. In some cases, the contrast between their expressed philosophy and practice in the classroom is due to their orientation. Because of previous experience in teaching regular grades, many teachers find it difficult to change their expectations of pupil achievement and to alter their methods. The lack of prepared materials for use with the mentally retarded and unrealistic expectations on the part of administrators, also contribute to the dilemma which surrounds curriculum development for the mentally retarded. In general, the inconsistencies in instructional practices found in special classes might be explained most readily in terms of the lack of a single proven approach to teaching the mentally retarded.

Unlike the third grade teacher who has access to well-researched and expertly designed texts, teachers' manuals, and supplemental materials, the special class teacher must rely on her own ability to modify and/or prepare materials. Certainly, materials used in the regular classes have value for the mentally retarded. However, it must be remembered that while in the regular classes, the retarded child failed to profit sufficiently from the same material. This child often brings to the special class negative attitudes towards the material he has been using, as well as similar attitudes toward school in general. The problem is further complicated by the limited scope of most programs for the retarded, and the difficulty of maintaining sequence in the skills taught to them. Much of the research that has been done on teaching the mentally retarded suggests they learn best through experience with concrete materials and meaningful repetition. In reality, no one approach seems to work effectively for all teachers. Consequently, the teacher tends to experiment with different methods and ultimately uses the one which works best for her. Such approaches range from a "watered-down" version of the regular curriculum to complete reliance on unit teaching. While special educators are sensitive to this situation, considerable difference of opinion continues to exist relative to the specific techniques most effective in teaching the mentally retarded. There is probably more agreement on the kinds of information that should be taught to the retarded and the type of social being he should become than there is on teaching the fundamentals of basic skills. It appears that much of the confusion centers on academic expectations which are realistic only in terms of the mentally retarded child's performance in the areas of reading and arithmetic. Competency in both skills is essential to independent living. Because of this, there is a tendency on the part of many teachers to initiate formal instruction too soon in these skills with the mentally retarded. They overlook the factor of readiness, and introduce concepts and tasks to the retarded before he is capable of coping with them. When this happens, emotional problems may develop, or the child merely learns unrelated parts of what should be sequential learning. The consequences of this error are great. First, learning under these conditions is inefficient; second, the techniques and materials used with the child who did not attain the appropriate level of readiness the first time will be less effective the second time.

If the purpose of special classes is to improve the instruction of retarded children, it is obvious that the curriculum is the key to the success of the program. In spite of the problems previously cited which tend to complicate curriculum planning for the mentally retarded, sound programs can be structured. The selection of a good teacher represents a major factor. The administrator is in a position to influence the direction and quality of the program. If a special education supervisor or a consultant knowledgeable in curriculum for the mentally retarded is not available, much of the responsibility for curriculum development will fall to building principals. The four following suggestions relate to the administrative influence on curriculum for the mentally retarded.

Every principal in the system should understand the relationship of special classes to the overall school program. They should also be acquainted with what takes place in classes for the mentally retarded. Principals of buildings in which special classes are housed should be well informed on the different approaches to educating retarded children. This can be accomplished through professional reading, visiting programs in other districts, or completing additional college preparation.

Principals should refrain from mandating the use of certain materials or techniques. He should work with the teacher in the selection of materials. It is not uncommon to find situations in which principals have selected a supply of currently available texts and required their use in the special class. The special class teacher may prefer other materials, but because of her subordinate role feels compelled to comply.

The teacher should not be given complete autonomy to structure her own program, even though she should have flexibility in the selection of materials and experimentation with techniques. It is extremely important that there be continuity and sequence throughout the total program of special classes. What is taught to the eight and ten-year-olds must prepare them for experiences at the eleven and thirteen-year level. Curriculum planning should be a staff endeavor.

A certain amount of flexibility is required on the part of administrators because the special class curriculum involves the frequent use of field trips, demonstrations, dramatizations, and the use of practical learning centers. For example, policies regarding a limited number of field trips per year may need to be relaxed in the case of special classes for the mentally retarded. Another example relates to the use of supplies. Since the teacher will rely more on teacher-made materials and modification of materials of the regular classroom teacher, his demands for supplies may be greater. On the other hand, he may make less use of basic texts and other commercial materials.

Following is a brief description of instructional programs for the educable mentally retarded at the elementary, junior high, and senior high levels. Since considerable reference throughout this chapter has been made to curriculum planning at the elementary and junior high levels, major attention will be given to secondary level programs. Educators in general have been slow to implement secondary level programs for the educable mentally retarded. This is unfortunate because the high school program represents the culminating level of the total program for the retarded. At this stage teachers should capitalize on previous training, and experiences relevant to the world of work should be provided. In discussing secondary programs for the mentally retarded, specific attention will be given to the organizational structure as well as to curriculum content.

Elementary

For purposes of discussion, the elementary level will refer to classes serving children from approximately six to twelve years of age. The age range in a given class may vary, depending upon the size of the school district and the number of classes. In many school districts educable children are not placed in special classes until they have spent two to three years in the regular class. When this is the case, they may have attained a state of readiness which makes formal instruction in the basic skill areas appropriate. However, in situations in which children are placed in the special class as young as six years of age, the initial emphasis of the curriculum should be in the area of social development, strengthening of large muscle coordination and improvement of communication skills. The young retarded child frequently enters school not having had many of the experiences of his normal peers. Emphasis must be given to providing these children opportunities to interact with other children, be exposed to a stimulating environment and to identify with adult figures other than their parents. The pre-academic stage for these children will be much longer than for children with average ability. This is due to their slower rate of mental and social development.

When the child shows indication of having achieved a level of readiness for instruction in basic skills, formalized instruction can be introduced. While it is important that the child attain competency in the basic skills at the elementary level, it must be recognized that he will probably be eight to eight and one-half years of age chronologically before he is ready to learn to read, and will progress at a slower rate from that point on than will his normal peers. Because his interest level may be above that of most material designed for the typical child with a mental age of six, considerable attention will need to be given to modifying materials as well as supplementing these with materials of a higher interest level.

The use of concrete examples and experiences is essential. Materials used with the retarded child must be made as meaningful and relevant as possible. This involves reliance on the child's frame of reference, which means the teacher must be cognizant of the child's background in order to build upon the knowledge and skills the child has attained.

Most special classes for the educable mentally retarded at the elementary level are self-contained, with the possible exception of special subjects such as art, music and physical education. In situations in which the special class teacher does not assume responsibility for these subjects, the nonacademic teachers are used, or the special class children are integrated in regular classes with children of their age level.

It should be noted that the breadth of experience at the elementary level for retarded children should not be less than that provided children in regular classes. It is essential that retarded children have many experiences in a variety of areas. Field trips offer one approach to bringing retarded children into social contact with elements of their environment which are difficult to replicate in the classroom.

Because of the limitations of much of the commercially-prepared material designed for regular classes, many special class teachers have found the use of life experience units effective in teaching the mentally retarded. Teaching basic skills can be made relevant through the utilization of units of work. The unit becomes primarily a tool for teaching skills and, secondly, a vehicle for teaching content. It should be noted that if experience units are to be used, the teacher must plan his units so that the skills taught through them are presented in sequence.

Junior High

At the junior high level, major attention is given to maximizing the child's abilities in basic skills. However, the orientation of instruction should lean toward the application of these skills with emphasis given to practical application. Children at this level experience many social and emotional demands which result in adjustment problems. The mentally retarded particularly need experiences which will help them develop socially. Although personal hygiene should receive attention throughout the educational program for retarded children, specific attention must be given at the junior high level. The area of sex education must be incorporated in the instructional program.

The heavy emphasis on application relates to the areas of basic science, social skills, arithmetic and vocational skills. Instruction relative to vocational attitudes and prevocational skills should also be introduced. This can be done through an emphasis on job opportunities and may take the form of guidance sessions in which pupils are given opportunities to explore their own ideas leading to vocations and to develop a perspective of work experience.

If the secondary program in which the junior high pupils will later participate requires them to move from class to class, they should be given this experience at the junior high level so they can cope with the situation successfully. In many cases, it has been found beneficial to arrange for visitations to the high school during the last year of the junior high program so that pupils can formulate views on the experiences they will encounter.

SECONDARY SCHOOL PROGRAM

Programming for educable mentally retarded youth at the secondary level has only recently begun to receive major attention from educators. Historically, special education for the retarded focused on children at the elementary level. The first classes established generally were for children nine to twelve years of age chronologically. These students were being confronted with the academic challenge of basic skills and were unable to cope with these demands. Administrators soon realized that their limitations were not remediable and that placement in a special class did not prepare them for later return to the regular system. As the children initially placed in the classes matured and younger children were enrolled, the age span increased and the need for additional levels of classes became apparent. In many districts the practice has been to provide special education for the youth until his sixteenth birthday or the legal limit for mandatory school attendance, then prematurely refer the youth to the vocational rehabilitation agency, encourage him to seek employment, or return him to the regular high school program where he eventually became a dropout. In some situations he was allowed to remain in the special class, or special provisions were made to tailor a modified educational program for him in the regular high school. Until recently, special education programs for the educable mentally retarded at the secondary level have been the exception.

Today educators are recognizing that if the skills of the retarded are to be maximized, the retarded youth must receive the benefit of a training program geared to preparing him for the world of work. With increased automation exerting a significant influence and the unskilled labor market rapidly diminishing, the training of the mentally retarded youth in employable skills requires an increased investment in educational programming. Longitudinal studies have demonstrated that the retarded can be productive, but that training is required; merely keeping the youth in a school setting is not sufficient. Vocational and social experiences appropriate to the ability, interest, and maturity of the mentally retarded youth must be provided. This means broadening the school program to include on-the-job training, practice in applying for a job, working with allied agencies in order to familiarize the retarded with agencies on which he can rely in times of need, and providing academic opportunities designed to reinforce vocational preparation.

Types of Existing Programs

Adjusted Program

Many districts, particularly small districts, attempt to program for the retarded youth through selective placement. They may group the lower functioning youth for basic skill subjects such as general math and communication skills, then rely upon regular class offerings to complete the program. The retarded are integrated in regular vocational classes, art, home economics, driver education, and possibly general science. Courses such as algebra, foreign language, history and geometry are excluded from the program. While the retarded may gain from this type of programming, such programs frequently result in many voids in his educational experiences and "social promotion" becomes the pattern. The primary problem centers around integrating groups of retarded youth into regular classes. Certainly some educable retarded youth functioning to near-capacity can profit from regular class placement. These youth should be given the opportunity to compete with their more able peers. However, a large per cent of the retarded are not able to keep up even with the lower track in the regular high school curriculum, so relying on regular classroom activities to comprise their educational program is impractical. When integration in the regular program is used as an alternative, the retarded youth's ability, understandings of the regular teacher, and attitudes of the "normal" peers must be considered.

Self-contained Classes

Experience with self-contained classes at the elementary and junior high levels has influenced a number of districts to maintain this pattern for the secondary program. Where the available number of eligible youth is only sufficient for one class and if a trained teacher can be employed, a self-contained unit can be structured to provide adequate experiences. In such cases it is advisable to make the regular industrial arts and home economics facilities available to the special class. Particular attention should also be given to individualized integration in regular classes. If there are youth in the special class with certain talents or sufficient ability to satisfactorily participate in selected regular classes, the opportunity should be afforded them. The major obstacle to developing a secondary program for a group of retarded youth through the self-contained approach is in organizing experiences with the variety and challenge to appeal to the teenager. Assigning a teacher to be responsible for a group throughout the day places him at a disadvantage. If this is the situation, daily activities should be organized to provide the students contact with other teachers for at least one period during the day. This gives the students a change of pace, and allows the special class teacher a planning period. The students need contact with other teachers; this additional interaction is part of the process of developing independence. Including the special class pupils in the regular physical education program with the regular students can help accomplish this goal.

Departmentalized Core Program

When there are enough eligible pupils to warrant several classes at the secondary level, there are certain advantages to the departmentalized core program. Some of these advantages are as follows.

1. The special class pupils can be assigned to regular home room classes. This reduces the social stigma often attributed to the special class, and also allows the special class teacher to have a regular home room, thus providing her an opportunity to have contact with a cross section of the student body.

2. Special class teachers can be assigned to teach in their primary area of competency. This reduces the demands resulting from preparing for three or four subject matter areas; it affords an opportunity to be more creative, and to focus on the individual needs of the pupil.

3. Having the pupils rotate classes according to the same time schedule as the regular high school pupils makes the differences in their program less apparent. It also helps them build independence.

4. Departmentalized programs offer flexibility in grouping. Pupils can be assigned to classes according to ability and major areas of need.

5. By offering several core areas (core areas refer to subjects such as vocational attitudes, communication skills, practical math) taught by special class teachers, there is more opportunity to develop scope to the program and at the same time provide some assurance that the sequence of experiences will be appropriate. Teachers responsible for multiple sessions of one or two core areas are in a better position to analyze the student's performance and structure learning experiences relative to the needs of the pupils.

An obvious requirement for departmentalized programs is a large population base; however, another prerequisite is a commitment to coordination. Because teachers will have responsibility for teaching one or two core areas rather than the full sequence, there is a definite need to coordinate the efforts of the respective teachers. One approach is to designate the responsibility of coordination to one of the teachers who possesses the necessary coordination skills. If a consultant for the mentally retarded or special education supervisor is available, he can assume this task. Because of the many duties assigned to principals, rarely are they in a position to devote the time required to adequately coordinate a departmentalized special education program within their building. It may be that a person such as the assistant principal who has sufficient background and has established rapport with the special class teachers can assume the coordination responsibilities.

Work-Study Programs

These programs for secondary age, educable mentally retarded youth are becoming very popular. In addition to providing continued experience in the practical application of basic skills, the youth is afforded an opportunity to gain experience on an actual job setting. The work experience may be provided in the community through agreement with local employers, or work settings within the school may be used. These might include the bus garage, janitorial work, laundry, cafeteria and grounds. The classroom experience includes an emphasis on practical mathematics, budgeting, applying for a job, using the services of employment and allied agencies, reading, and related domestic skills. Considerable time is also devoted to exploring the problems encountered by the student during his work experiences.

Organization of Work-Study Programs

While there is no set pattern for the organization of Work-Study Programs, there are some structures which experience has proved to be workable. There are many reasons why a district will choose one organizational structure over another. These reasons generally relate to local policies, precedence, or biases on the part of staff members. The following suggestions are offered as guidelines to be considered in organizing such a program. They can be modified to meet the demands of the local district.

1. The program should be for a period of at least three years in duration. Special classes should be an integral part of the regular secondary program.

2. Special pupils should be assigned regular home rooms.
3. The instructional program should be organized on a core basis with the core areas taught by special class teachers.
4. A coordinator should be appointed to be responsible for liaison activities between the school and participating employers; a full-time coordinator may be required depending on the number of pupils involved. Otherwise a teacher may be given free time to serve as the coordinator.
5. The work program should be considered as an essential part of the school program.
6. Special class pupils should be included in extra-curricular activities, physical education and other regular classes when their performance warrants such placement.
7. Liaison with a written working agreement should be established with the local vocational rehabilitation office.

Samples of Instructional Programs

SOPHOMORE YEAR

The student should spend full time in the core program except for field trips to implement work orientation. Students with considerable maturity might be given limited work experience during their sophomore year. For the majority of students this will be initiated during the junior year.

Classes should include:

1. Communication skills*
2. Occupations*
3. Practical mathematics*
4. Social practices*
5. Physical education
6. Practical arts*

Frequent group discussions involving seniors and juniors should be held to introduce the sophomores to the kinds of problems and demands they can expect to encounter during their work experiences.

---

* Core classes which provide the major component of educational experience.

Counseling sessions with a counselor or coordinator should be arranged as indicated by the interests of the pupil.

JUNIOR YEAR

The student should be given experience in at least three different work settings during his junior year. The length of the work experience should be at least two hours per day but should not exceed a half day.

The school program should include:

1. Communication skills with emphasis on reading the newspaper, plus other reading material related to the student's work experience
2. Occupations with an emphasis on employer-employee relations
3. Practical mathematics stressing budgeting of salary (introduction of payroll deductions)
4. Social practices
5. Physical education
6. Practical arts

SENIOR YEAR

During the senior year, work experience should receive the major attention. Each student should receive a minimum of two different work experiences, and at least a half day should be spent on the job. This can be increased as the youth shows proficiency and capability for full-time employment.

Classes include:

1. Practical math with an emphasis on social security, income tax, banking, insurance and workmen's compensation
2. Practical arts, including home economics for the girls and industrial arts for the boys
3. Social practices
4. Continued emphasis on communication skills
5. Group counseling sessions with other students and representatives of community agencies should be scheduled as part of the program. Participating agencies might include

vocational rehabilitation, state employment service, organized labor, and selected employers
6. Physical education

Students should not be assigned work experience full-time if they have major weaknesses in the core areas.

Involvement of Community Agencies

Since many educable, mentally retarded youth will have need for services offered by the state's employment service and/or the vocational rehabilitation center at different times in their lives, it is important that they become acquainted with the purposes of these agencies. Both agencies also have much to offer in the establishment of Work-Study Programs; representatives of these agencies should be invited to participate in planning the Work-Study Program. In many states cooperative programs can be developed between the local school district and the state's division of vocational rehabilitation to help coordinate the Work-Study Program. Through such cooperative ventures the student receives the benefit of vocational counseling and can identify with the rehabilitation agency, thus making later contact much easier.

Service clubs and fraternal organizations can be of assistance in finding work experience opportunities. Prior to contacting such groups, school personnel should have in mind the kinds of job situations which are most beneficial. Policies regarding the relationship between the school and the employer must be developed. Decisions will need to be made pertaining to salaries, insurance, supervision and work scheduling. Policies relating to these subjects should be established prior to actively soliciting work experiences.

General Considerations

It is not uncommon for a student to encounter success on a job setting, then decide to continue working but to drop out of school. Unless the student happens to be a senior and functioning at a high level, he should be encouraged to stay in the school program. Because such situations do occur, it is particularly important that students understand the importance of gaining experience in several work settings. They must also be made to comprehend that the work experience is training and that the major purpose *at this stage* is not to earn money. Cooperating employers may be able to help persuade the students to continue the school program if the situation arises.

If work experiences are to be sought in union shops, agreement on the conditions of the training program should be established in advance with labor representatives. Many employers will raise questions regarding apprenticeships and union membership. Arrangements can be worked out with labor representatives to accommodate the training program.

Although employers should accept students with the understanding that the program is for training purposes, they must also assume some responsibility for supervision of the work experience. On-the-job supervision should be supplemented by the coordinator from the school. Unless the student is given appropriate supervision, the work experience does not meet the conditions of a training program.

Students completing the requirements of secondary special class programs should be entitled to participate in all commencement exercises. The awarding of diplomas is handled in different ways. Some award a special diploma which includes a statement that the youth has fulfilled the requirements of the Work-Study Program. Others are awarded a certificate of attendance. Some districts issue regular diplomas that indicate the special conditions under which they were granted.

Modifications of the Work-Study Concept

Many districts with small enrollments employ the basic features of a Work-Study Program on a limited scale. For example, students enrolled in self-contained secondary classes can be assigned work experiences on a part-time basis. Under such circumstances, demands for work-training settings would be small; it may be that only seven or eight would need to be involved in work experiences during a given year. In other situations, a number of small districts may organize a cooperative Work-Study Program and centralize their secondary classes. Under these conditions the county board of education or an intermediate unit might be approached to supply a coordinator; or a coordinator can be jointly employed by the participating districts.

Extra-Curricular Activities

Extra-curricular activities are a definite part of secondary education. When a pupil is placed in a special class for the mentally retarded, these activities and related special education services become the total educational program, just as the regular program is a total program for the "normal" youth. Because of this, there is the ever-present danger of overlooking the extra-curricular activities which are particularly important to youth at the secondary age level. While some special interest groups can be organized within the confines of a special class structure, the number of pupils and the varying interests of these students preclude the development of an adequate extra-curricular activity program for the retarded youth alone. Even if the number of mentally retarded youth were sufficient, there would be little justification for the practice. These youth frequently have interests similar to their "normal" high school peers. Talent in the arts and abilities in athletics are not rare among educable mentally retarded. Every attempt should be made to include the retarded youth in regular extra-curricular activities.

Some administrators have questioned the advisability of allowing educable mentally retarded youth to participate in interscholastic athletic competition. This concern usually centers around the determination of eligibility. In some cases, the situation has been resolved by recognizing special education as the educational program designed by the schools for the retarded pupil. If he is passing at a satisfactory level the classes to which he has been assigned, then he is declared eligible. This is the same basis as is required for the "normal" youth. It is obviously unrealistic to require the retarded youth to meet the standards set for students with considerably more ability. To meet these standards he, of course, would have to be an over-achiever.

The disproportionate attention given to secondary programs in this chapter is because the practice of providing elementary and junior high special classes is generally widespread. Administrators must recognize their obligation to giving leadership in the development of secondary programs. *A willingness to start an elementary special class should be a commitment to the establishment of a secondary level program;* otherwise the elementary program has only limited meaning.

TRAINABLE MENTALLY RETARDED

Public school programming for the trainable mentally retarded has only recently begun to receive the attention of school administrators. The trainable child represents a group which ten years ago typically was not served in the public schools. They remained at home, attended privately operated day schools, or resided in institutions for the mentally retarded. Their severe intellectual limitations and frequent physical problems dictated a kind of curriculum that educators were unaccustomed to providing, and which many felt was beyond the expectations of the public schools. However, as classes increased for the educable mentally retarded, active concern for programs to serve the trainable mentally retarded was generated among parents and interested persons. Parent-operated classes began to appear, and it became apparent that classes could provide considerable benefit to the child and his family. The focus soon turned to the public schools as the logical public agency to provide this vital portion of the continuum of care for the trainable mentally retarded.

Many districts were hesitant but legislation and community support prevailed. Today classes for the trainable are considered an integral part of comprehensive public school programs. Whether or not a particular administrator favors a public school role in serving the trainable mentally retarded is no longer a justification for withholding support for their development. The current issue is: How can educational programs best be structured to maximize the gains for the child and his family?

In general, the term "trainable mentally retarded" is applied to those persons whose measured I.Q. is in the 30-50 range. While I.Q. should not be the single criteria for determining eligibility for placement, it does serve as a reasonable frame of reference.

Communication skills, social development and general health should also be considered. As an adult, the trainable mentally retarded may develop semi-independence but will probably require continued supervision. Many will profit from the services of a sheltered workshop; others will be capable of group living outside the home; still others will require institutionalization.

Identification and Placement

Unlike the educable retarded the task of identification of the trainable retarded is not a matter of screening from among the public school enrollment. Rarely will the trainable mentally retarded be found attending regular classes beyond kindergarten or first grade. Sources of referrals include parent groups, medical doctors, mental health clinics, social welfare agencies and public health nurses. Their retardation is generally obvious. The difficulty lies in determining their major strengths and the particular skills they are capable of developing.

Most states have requirements for eligibility. The states' departments of public instruction generally provide guidelines for the establishment of classes. In addition to the I.Q. criterion, districts are often encouraged to require that the child be able to communicate his wants, be toilet trained, and possess basic self-help skills. Although these requirements appear reasonable, they should be judiciously applied. It is not uncommon to find a child who is not toilet trained, but who accomplishes the task easily under the management of a teacher or matron. The mother may have been unsuccessful because she began to train the child too early, or the parent-child relationship was too emotionally involved. This example is cited as an appeal for experimentation and flexibility in admission requirements for young trainable mentally retarded children. Initial placement should be on a trial basis.

Classroom

Although the recommended maximum enrollment per class is ten to twelve, the kinds of activities incorporated in the curriculum require a space allocation similar to a regular class. This would be approximately 900 square feet. The room should have the basic attributes of good lighting, pleasant colors and safety features typical of good elementary classrooms. For younger trainable mentally retarded children a self-contained unit offers many advantages for the curriculum. This means including in the classroom a sink and restroom, as well as facilities for modest food preparation. Many classes of the trainable mentally retarded are held in facilities outside the regular school campuses. Assuming that the structure has been remodeled or designed for the class, the facility might well meet the needs of the children. Concern for socialization among the trainable mentally retarded children and their normal peers is not as crucial as it is with the educable mentally retarded group. Should the class be held in a regular building, the room should be located near the entrance or have a private entrance so that frequent field trips or use of outdoor experiences will not interrupt school activity in the building. The incidence of children with physical handicaps and coordination problems will be much greater among the trainable mentally retarded than other groups. Thus, consideration should be given to a non-slip floor surface, and care should be taken in the selection of furniture.

Because the incidence of children in the trainable mentally retarded range is relatively small (an estimated .5 per cent) a school district with an enrollment of approximately 8,000 is required to have sufficient trainable children to offer classes on at least three levels. Of course, the population base can be extended by involving adjacent districts or establishing a county-wide program. In many rural areas the maximum number, even on a county basis, may not be greater than twenty-five to thirty. In such situations the level of classes may be limited to two, with considerable differentiation in the curriculum experiences being made within the class.

It should be noted that through cooperation with allied social agencies, residential facilities, or foster home programs on a five-day-a-week basis, the number of children available for programming can be increased. Such a venture, of course, necessitates that the child be separated from the family during the week. In the future, as preschool and vocational programs are undertaken, more consideration will need to be given to this approach.

Assuming that approximately thirty-five children within the trainable mentally retarded level are available for grouping, three different ability levels can be structured. The child's social development, his maturity and physical development must be considered in establishing criteria for transfer from one level to another. A brief description of the curriculum emphasis at each level follows.

CURRICULUM FOR THE TRAINABLE RETARDED
Level I

The primary emphasis of the first level is on basic self-help skills and socialization. Dressing oneself, feeding, and following directions receive considerable attention. Many trainable children will come to school with limited previous contact with children or adults other than those in their immediate family. Their realm of experience will be limited; the teacher will devote considerable time to structuring activities which will stimulate the child to interact with his environment. Communication within the context of expressing wants should also be an integral part of the school experience at this level. Special attention is given to the development of large muscle coordination and motor skills.

Level II

Emphasis on the development of self-help continues; however, there is a trend away from the basic skills of dressing and feeding oneself to self-help skills related to care of clothing and personal hygiene. Considerable attention is given to language development. The focus is on enhancing the child's willingness to speak and improving general quality of language used to express himself. The concern is not necessarily for articulation. Reading related to the recognition of crucial words such as safety signs, labels and names is introduced. Basic number concepts becomes a part of the curriculum. The outcome of arithmetic experiences at this level includes an understanding of numbers from one to ten, comprehension of quantity differences, and an ability to discriminate between large and small and varied shaped objects.

In the area of social development, attention is given to property rights, respect for authority and the formulation of general attitudes. The latter, of course, should be inherent in the child's training which begins prior to school; however, until he begins identifying with a group and participating in group interaction, any understanding of the consequence of certain acts is difficult for him to achieve.

Level III

At this level the curriculum should include activities geared toward the use of vocational skills. Prevocational experiences for the trainable mentally retarded, while not the same as for the educable or normal youth, should be work-oriented. The specific experience to be incorporated into the curriculum at this particular level will be influenced by the types of community resources in which the youth will participate after leaving the school experience. If a sheltered workshop with a terminal setting is available, the third level of the program should be coordinated with the activities provided through this shop. Simulated work tasks can be conducted in class culminating with a child's work experience in a sheltered workshop. If the only resource available to the youth (following completion of the school program) is the home and vocational experiences obtained for him by his family, then the orientation of the program might be more in terms of developing domestic skills which can be applied at home or outside the home under supervision.

There are some basic attitudes and skills which have general application for the trainable mentally retarded later in life. These must be stressed in the education program at different levels. Included are the following:

1. Ability to follow directions
2. Ability to complete a task
3. General concept of time
4. Ability to move about in neighborhood and community
5. Understanding of protective resources

6. Competence in practical arts relative to domestic chores
7. Limited facility with conversational speech

In general, the curriculum should be comprised of experiences which bring the child into meaningful contact with his environment. What is obvious to the teacher, parent, and normal peers must be brought to the attention of the trainable mentally retarded. His curiosity must be stimulated to the extent that he gains reinforcement from the routine activities of daily living. As he is introduced to new experiences or familiar tasks from a different frame of reference, every attempt should be made to maximize the relevance of the experience. School for the trainable mentally retarded is not comprised of books, desks and recitation. Instead, school means participating in activities which will facilitate the child's development of personal and social skills related to self-sufficiency. Granted, minimal reading and arithmetic skills cannot be ruled out as a possibility for development of the trainable mentally retarded child; however, an over-emphasis on the teaching of these skills at the expense of developing self-help skills, communications, and social skills must be avoided.

In summarizing this brief description of educational programs for the trainable mentally retarded, it should be noted that special classes for the trainable attract the attention of many community groups. Affiliate organizations of the National Association for Retarded Children represent a significant source of help. Others include service groups and church organizations. Many such groups view the class (or classes) as a worthy project. The class soon becomes the recipient of gifts and donations. While the public relations element of these gestures is valuable, unless policies are established regarding the procedurs for donations and priorities in terms of the kinds of gifts which are appropriate, many problems may arise. One approach is to assist the teacher in developing a list of materials and equipment which she can use effectively in her program and make it available upon request to interested groups. It is also advantageous to have gifts donated to the school in general, for use in the class for the trainable, rather than directed specifically to the class for the trainable mentally retarded.

As comprehensive community programming for the trainable mentally retarded becomes a reality, clinics, sheltered workshops, group living homes, day care centers, and extended care facilities will become available. When this stage is reached, the public school program will be playing a valuable role in the continuum of care for this population of the mentally retarded. At the same time the responsibility of the educator will increase; he will need to know the language of the various disciplines involved. Programming for the trainable mentally retarded offers a real challenge to public school administrators because the successful implementation of a good program will necessitate interaction with the fields of rehabilitation, medicine, social welfare, and employment.

SUMMARY

The popularity of special classes for the mentally retarded indicates that educators generally accept this approach as being realistic and practical. This does not mean that equal educational opportunity for the mentally retarded is merely a matter of organization. Rather, the validity of this approach must be measured in terms of the effectiveness of the instructional methods and the materials used in the special classes. Reported research, comparing the achievement of retarded in special classes with similar children in regular classes, suggests that academically there may be little difference. Such findings should be sufficient evidence to encourage administrators to support their commitment to the retarded in special classes by seeking trained teachers, providing appropriate materials and by structuring programs with a full range of educational experience. Only through the provision of a sequential program can the retarded be assured of equal educational opportunity.

While staff, materials, and facilities can be purchased, administrative support and direction must result from administrators with insight who view special education for the mentally retarded as an integral part of a comprehensive school program. Underlying this perspective must be the employment of evaluative techniques which result in continued progress toward improvement. The grouping of children into special classes because of intellectual limitations enhances the teaching of children in the regular classes; however, this does not compensate for a less adequate job with the mentally retarded. Administrators often need to be reminded that once a child is placed in a special class, the special class curriculum tends to become the child's educational program, and rarely does he find his way back to regular classes. If this is the case, then there must be a strong commitment toward paralleling the regular class system with structured sequential special classes through the secondary level.

Appendix A

SUMMARY, CONCLUSIONS, AND RECOMMENDATIONS OF THE LOS ANGELES STUDY*

IN this chapter, the study is closed with an interpretation of the findings summarized at this point from the overall perspective of the complete research report. Following each summary are the conclusions and recommendations for the use of the data obtained and reported in the study.

I. STATEMENT OF THE PROBLEM AND PROCEDURE

The primary purpose of the investigation was to determine recommendations by specialists regarding the definition, function, organization, and administration of the special education program. In order to accomplish the stated objective, it was decided that the most effective method of acquiring such information was by a questionnaire technique.

Accordingly, questionnaires were sent to forty-eight state departments of education; twenty-six universities which had a department of special education headed by a director or coordinator; and, 117 professors of school administration. The total percentage of usable replies received were as follows: (1) 82 per cent from state departments of education; (2) 69 per cent from special education experts; and, (3) 50 per cent from professors of school administration.

Statistical treatment of data was limited to classification, tabulation, and computation of percentages.

---

* In 1959, Dr. Ellis A. Jarvis, then the Superintendent of Schools of the Los Angeles City School Districts, recommended to the Board of Education that "funds be allocated for the purpose of initiating a study that would present data regarding the definition, function, organization, and administration of a Special Education program." The study was an excellent one, and the author is indebted to Dr. Jarvis, Dr. Frank Hodgson (who conducted the study) and the Los Angeles Board of Education for permission to reprint Chapter IV of this study.

II. DEFINITION OF SPECIAL EDUCATION

Defining the Term Special Education

Summary

1. Questionnaire respondents indicated that the following categories should be included in defining Special Education.

   a. Blind
   b. Partially seeing
   c. Deaf
   d. Hard of hearing
   e. Lip reading
   f. Speech correction
   g. Cerebral palsied
   h. Orthopedically handicapped
   i. Chronic medical problems
   j. Mentally retarded
   k. Mentally deficient
   l. Emotionally and/or socially disturbed
   m. Gifted
   n. Hospital teaching
   o. Home teaching

2. Questionnaire respondents indicated that the following categories should not be defined as Special Education:

   a. Remedial reading
   b. Remedial arithmetic
   c. Foreign adjustment classes
   d. Corrective physical education

3. The above summary should be qualified by the following factors:

   a. Although a majority of professors of school administration indicated that the categories chronic medical problems and mentally deficient should be included in the term Special Education, reservation was expressed by a thirty-three per cent negative response.
   b. Professors of school administration indicated serious ques-

tion as to the inclusion of the gifted category in defining Special Education. Forty-seven per cent recommended inclusion and forty-three per cent recommended exclusion of the gifted category in defining Special Education.

c. When a composite was made of all returns, twenty-nine per cent of the respondents indicated a negative response to the inclusion of the mentally deficient in defining Special Education as opposed to fifty-nine per cent recommending inclusion.

Conclusions and Recommendations

1. It is recommended that the summary presentation of data indicated in item No. 1 be accepted as the descriptive definition of the Special Education program.
2. Categories listed in the broad definition of the term "Special Education" are not synonymous with Special Education department assigned responsibilities. Categories of Special Education to be placed in the department of Special Education must be decided not only in terms of definition, but also administrative framework structure.

Special Education Categories to Be Included in Department of Special Education

Summary

1. Respondents were agreed that the following Special Education categories should be the direct responsibility of a department of Special Education:

   a. Blind
   b. Partially seeing
   c. Deaf
   d. Hard of hearing
   e. Lip reading
   f. Speech correction
   g. Cerebral palsied
   h. Orthopedically handicapped
   i. Mentally retarded
   j. Chronic medical problems

    k. Emotionally and/or socially disturbed

    l. Hospital teaching

    m. Home teaching

2. Questionnaire respondents indicated that the following categories of Special Education should not be the responsibility of a department of Special Education:

    a. Remedial reading

    b. Remedial arithmetic

    c. Foreign adjustment

    d. Corrective physical education

3. State department respondents and specialists tended to recommend that the mentally deficient and the gifted should be included as categories of responsibility for a department of Special Education. A majority of professors of school administration indicated a negative response for the inclusion of the latter two categories in the department of Special Education.

Conclusions and Recommendations

1. Categories of Special Education to be assigned a department of Special Education will be partially determined by the administrative structure. Based on the study, there are two possible administrative framework structures that would be compatible to the Los Angeles City School District, namely:

    a. A separate department of Special Education with line authority over Special Education schools and staff relationship over centers.

    b. A Special Education department attached to the operational section (Deputy Superintendent) with advisory and supervisory relationship to District Assistant Superintendents, principals, and teaching personnel.

2. Categories of Special Education that should be the responsibility of a separate department of Special Education with line authority leadership may include the following areas:

    a. Blind school

    b. Deaf school

   c. Crippled and delicate schools

   d. Speech correction

   e. Lip reading

   f. Hospital teaching

   g. Home teaching

Special Education categories which are organized in terms of classes and centers would necessitate a staff relationship with the department of Special Education to avoid dual authority. Thus the following categories would be under the leadership of the local District Assistant Superintendent with advisory and supervisory aid available from the department of Special Education as requested:

   a. Point I program

   b. Hard of hearing (if classes are formed)

   c. Partially seeing

   d. Emotionally and socially disturbed

   e. Gifted

   f. General remedial programs (reading, arithmetic, etc.)

   g. Foreign adjustment classes

If the mentally deficient program is expanded, the department of Special Education should be given "line" authority over Point II schools.

At the present time, where the mentally deficient program is experimental, the Special Education department should have only advisory and supervisory relationship with the Point II program.

3. Categories of Special Education that should be included in a department of Special Education structured for a "staff" relationship with schools and centers of Special Education may include the following areas:

   a. Blind

   b. Partially seeing

   c. Deaf

   d. Hard of hearing

   e. Lip reading

    f. Speech correction
    g. Crippled and delicate
    h. Mentally retarded
    i. Emotionally and socially disturbed
    j. Gifted
    k. Hospital teaching
    l. Home teaching

The mentally deficient would remain undesignated until the experimental program has been evaluated.

Education of the foreign born and all remedial classes would be the responsibility of the operational academic supervisors.

III. SCHOOL DISTRICT RESPONSIBILITY AND PER-PUPIL LOAD

School District Responsibility for Providing Educational Opportunity to Physically and Mentally Handicapped Children

Summary

1. Questionnaire respondents were agreed that educational opportunity and facilities should be provided by a city school district for the following categories of Special Education:

    a. Blind
    b. Partially seeing
    c. Deaf
    d. Hard of hearing
    e. Lip reading
    f. Speech correction
    g. Crippled and delicate
    h. Mentally retarded
    i. Emotionally and/or socially disturbed

2. Special Education experts and state department of education respondents indicated by a majority of two-to-one that school districts should be responsible for providing preschool educational opportunity for the following categories:

    j. Preschool blind
    k. Preschool deaf
    l. Preschool cerebral palsied

Professors of school administration indicated that school districts should not be responsible for providing preschool education opportunities for exceptional children. By a two-to-one majority, professors of school administration stated that it was not the responsibility of the school district to provide facilities and educational opportunities for the following categories:

j. Preschool blind
k. Preschool deaf
l. Preschool cerebral palsied (28% yes; 53% no)

3. Respondents were requested in two different sections of the questionnaire to indicate whether the public school should be responsible for providing the facilities for training children who range in I.Q. from zero to fifty.*

Where the question was isolated as an item by itself, a majority of more than two to one of the specialists and professors of school administration indicated that the public schools should not be responsible for training the mentally deficient.

Slightly over half (55%) of the state department of education respondents recommended that the public schools should be responsible for training mentally deficient children.

Conclusions and Recommendations

1. The Los Angeles City School District should continue to provide services to all categories of Special Education including preschool deaf and crippled.
2. The merits or advisability of training the mentally deficient should be determined primarily on research data obtained from the current pilot study. Public school responsibility for training Point II children should be carefully evaluated.
3. The possible use of home teachers to aid parents in training mentally deficient pupils may be worthy of future study.

Suggested Pupil Norm for Each Category of Special Education

Summary

1. More than one-half of the state department of education re-

---

* If the question had defined the term "mentally deficient" as a child with an I.Q. of from 30 to 50, the conclusions might be considerably different.

spondents indicated that the current Los Angeles pupil-norm for the following Special Education categories is too high:

a. Emotionally and/or socially disturbed
b. Mentally deficient
c. Speech correction
d. Orthopedically handicapped

State department of education respondents also indicated concern regarding the norm for lip reading.

2. More than one-half of the Special Education experts indicated that the current Los Angeles norm for the following Special Education categories is too high:

a. Emotionally and/or socially disturbed
b. Preschool deaf

Specialists also indicated concern regarding the norm for school age deaf, mentally retarded, and preschool blind.

3. Professors of school administration stated that the suggested (Los Angeles) pupil norm for each category of Special Education was satisfactory. The suggested norm figure receiving the greatest concern as reflected by a negative response was the area of the mentally retarded.

Conclusions and Recommendations

1. In evaluating the summary, it is important to recognize that the Los Angeles School District provides matron assistance for each teacher in the care of the mentally deficient, crippled, and delicate.

However, further study should be made to evaluate the need for a norm cushion for the cerebral palsied crippled classification. The present Los Angeles norm requires a minimum of 15 pupils per teacher; the state allows a maximum of 15 pupils per teacher. In order to classify a classroom as cerebral palsied, it is necessary to have a majority of cerebral palsied cases registered. In instances where there are eight cerebral palsied pupils and seven orthopedically crippled pupils, one cerebral palsied withdrawal could require a change of classification to "orthopedically handicapped." This change would require conforming to a norm of eighteen.

2. The Welfare Room concept in Los Angeles places emphasis on education adjustment rather than individual psychiatric therapy. Children who are unable to adjust to a flexible curriculum and a more permissive environment within a group situation are excluded. The revised minimum norm of twelve pupils per teacher adopted in 1960 would seem to be satisfactory on the basis of purpose and function of the Welfare Room.

3. The present norm for training the mentally deficient would seem to be entirely satisfactory.*

4. It is recommended that further study be given to possible reduction of the teacher norm for speech correction and lip reading. There is evidence, both in the Field Report and the Questionnaire Survey, that the present norm of 150 children a year per teacher in speech correction, and 140 children per teacher in lip reading may be too high.

5. All other categories of Special Education are concluded to have a norm sufficiently satisfactory to offer a strong education program.

IV. PUPIL PLACEMENT

Assignment of Responsibility for Final Decision

Regarding Pupil Placement

Summary

State department of education respondents, Special Education experts, and professors of school administration were agreed that final authority for pupil placement should be the responsibility of an educator. It was notable that thirty per cent of the respondents wrote a comment indicating recommendation for a team or group approach. A total of three per cent of the respondents recommended that medical or psychiatric personnel should be responsible for final decisions regarding pupil placement.

---

* Satisfaction was registered by the principal of Bellevue School regarding the pupil norm. (See Field Survey Report.)

Conclusions and Recommendations

1. The following conclusions and recommendations are based on an administrative structure whereby the director of Special Education is vested with "line" authority:

   a. The final decision regarding pupil placement and/or exclusion should be assigned to a director of Special Education in instances where decision involves pupil placement or exclusion in or from Special Education *schools*.

   b. All schools with Special Education classes may refer difficult pupil placement or exclusion cases to the director of Special Education for advisement upon recommendation of the Assistant Superintendent. Final decision and authority resides with the Associate Superintendent of the Division.

2. The following conclusions and recommendations are based on an administrative structure whereby the director of Special Education has "staff" relationship with Special Education schools and classes:

   All schools with Special Education classes and Special Education schools may refer difficult pupil placement or exclusion cases to the director of Special Education for advisement upon recommendation of the District Assistant Superintendent. Final decision and authority in all pupil placement cases resides with the Associate Superintendent of the Division.

Recommended Pupil Placement Organizational Plan

Summary

1. An analysis of data found general agreement among the respondents for the development of a centralized plan for pupil placement.
2. State department of education respondents indicated preference for a centralized pupil placement plan by a majority of more than two to one.
3. Specialists and professors of school administration indicated preference for a centralized pupil placement plan by slightly less than a two to one majority.

Conclusions and Recommendations

1. The following conclusions and recommendations are based on an administrative structure whereby the director of Special Education is vested with "line" authority:

   a. Pupil placement and exclusion in *schools* of Special Education should be centralized and controlled by the director of Special Education in terms of line authority. Operational processing for pupil placement would be decentralized for deaf, hard of hearing, blind, partial seeing, and crippled children.

      Each school for the physically handicapped would formulate an Admissions Committee to evaluate and examine children referred for possible placement. Referrals for Special Education services would be made by private and regular school physicians. The Admissions Committee would be comprised of (1) the Special Education school physician, (2) school principal, and (3) a Special Education psychologist acting in behalf of the director of Special Education. The Admissions Committee would jointly decide on pupil placement in a Special Education school, center, or return to a regular school. All pupil placements in Special Education schools or centers would be "trial placements" only, and subject to re-evaluation by the committee on the recommendation of the school principal and teacher concerned.

      It is also recommended that a Diagnostic Clinic be created to process all difficult pupil placement and/or exclusion cases where there is parent disagreement with the Admission Clinic recommendations. The Diagnostic Clinic would act as a Board of Appeal and would be formed as needed. The Board would be comprised of the following individuals: (1) Director of Special Education; (2) psychologist attached to the Department of Special Education; (3) examining physician from the Health and Medical Section; and (4) the school principal concerned. The Diagnostic Clinic recommendations would be considered final and approved by the director of Special Education. Further review of the case could be made only by the General Superintendent.

Centralized control over hospital and home teachers would also be the responsibility of the director of Special Education and administered by principals in his department. Lip reading and speech correction personnel would be under the direct authority of the Special Education director.

b. Schools containing Special Education *classes* would be under the direct control of the Assistant Superintendent. Pupil placement for the hard of hearing and partially seeing would be evaluated and processed at the nearest appropriate physically handicapped school by the Admissions Committee. Final placement must be approved by the District Assistant Superintendent for all assignments to Special Education classes.

Pupil placement, exclusions, and processing of the emotionally and/or socially disturbed, remedial classes, mentally retarded, foreign adjustment, and gifted would be processed on a district level.

District superintendents would be responsible for the above mentioned programs in their own districts.

Advisement, further pupil physical and psychiatric examinations, and supervisory aid would be available from the Department of Special Education upon request of the Assistant Superintendent.

Lip reading and speech correction education services would be available as requested from the Department of Special Education.

2. The following conclusions and recommendations are based on an administrative structure whereby the director of Special Education has been given "staff" relationship with Special Education schools and classes.

a. Pupil placement and exclusion would be decentralized. Routine pupil placement cases would be processed on a district level and approved by the District Assistant Superintendent.

b. Formulation of an Admissions Committee would be developed at each physically handicapped school as described in the plan for line authority assignment of responsibility to the Department of Special Education.

c. Pupil assignment responsibility may be delegated to the director of Special Education by Assistant Superintendents. However, final authority for all pupil placements resides with the district superintendents with final authority assigned to the Division Associate Superintendent.

d. A Diagnostic Clinic would be formulated to process all difficult pupil placement and/or exclusion cases. Use of this Clinic would be available as requested by assistant superintendents.

V. PUPIL ORGANIZATION

Pupil Organization Plans Recommended by Respondents

Summary

1. State department of education respondents, specialists, and professors of school administration were found to be in agreement relative to giving highest frequency to the following pupil organization plans:

   a. Elementary deaf — Partial Segregation
   b. Secondary deaf — Cooperative Plan
   c. Secondary crippled and delicate — Cooperative Plan
   d. Elementary mentally deficient — Segregated Plan
   e. Secondary mentally deficient — Segregated Plan
   f. Elementary mentally retarded — Partial Segregation

2. State department of education respondents and professors of school administration gave highest frequency to the Cooperative Plan for educating elementary hard of hearing pupils. Specialists gave highest frequency to the use of a Resource Room for educating the elementary hard of hearing pupil.

3. Specialists and state department respondents gave highest frequency to the use of a Resource Room for educating the secondary hard of hearing pupil. Professors of school administration gave highest frequency to the Cooperative Plan.

4. Respondent categories differed in the pupil organization plan given highest frequency for education of the elementary blind pupil. State department of education respondents gave highest frequency to the Cooperative Plan; specialists gave highest frequency to the Partial Segregation Plan; and, professors of school administration gave highest frequency to the Segregated Plan.

5. State department of education respondents and specialists gave highest frequency to the use of a Resource Room for educating the secondary blind student. Professors of school administration gave equal frequency to the Segregated Plan, Partially Segregated Plan, and Cooperative Plan for educating the secondary deaf student.

6. State department of education respondents and professors of school administration gave highest frequency to the Cooperative Plan for educating the elementary partial seeing pupil. Specialists gave highest frequency to the use of a Resource Room.

7. State department of education respondents and specialists were in agreement in giving highest frequency to the use of a Resource Room for educating the secondary partial seeing pupils. Professors of school administration gave highest frequency to the Cooperative Plan.

8. State department of education respondents and specialists gave highest frequency to the Partial Segregation Plan for educating the emotionally and/or socially disturbed child. Professors of school administration gave highest frequency to the Cooperative Plan.

9. State department of education respondents and professors of school administration gave highest frequency to the Cooperative Plan for educating the emotionally and/or socially disturbed secondary student. Specialists gave highest frequency to the Partial Segregation Plan.

10. State department of education respondents and professors of school administration gave highest frequency to the Cooperative Plan for educating the crippled elementary pupil. Specialists gave highest frequency to a Partial Segregation Plan.

11. Specialists were strongly in favor of a Cooperative Plan for educating the secondary mentally retarded student. State department of education respondents gave equal frequency to the Partial Segregation Plan and the Cooperative Plan. Professors of school administration gave highest frequency to the Partial Segregation Plan.

Conclusions and Recommendations

1. It may be concluded, for the purpose of this study, that for a majority of children the pupil organization plan receiving highest frequency in each category of Special Education represents the most suitable organization plan for a given handicap. It may not be concluded that a given organization plan is the best, e.g. ideal, or that all children would profit equally from a given form of pupil organization, or that any one form of pupil organization is "significantly superior" to the form of organization receiving the second highest number of frequencies.

2. Presented below is the pupil organization plan used for educating exceptional children in Los Angeles together with the organization plan receiving highest frequency as found by a composite of questionnaire returns.

LOS ANGELES QUESTIONNAIRE

DEAF
Elementary	Partial Segregation and Segregated	Partial Segregation
Secondary	Cooperative Plan	Cooperative Plan

BLIND
Elementary	Partial Segregation	Partial Segregation
Secondary	Resource Room	Resource Room

HARD OF HEARING
Elementary	Partial Segregation and Segregated	Cooperative
Secondary	Resource Room	Resource Room

PARTIAL SEEING
Elementary	Cooperative Plan	Cooperative Plan
Secondary	Resource Room	Cooperative Plan

EMOTIONALLY AND/OR SOCIALLY DISTURBED
Elementary	Cooperative Plan	Cooperative Plan
Secondary	Cooperative and Segregated	Cooperative Plan

CRIPPLED
Elementary	Segregated	Cooperative Plan
Secondary	Segregated and Cooperative Plan	Cooperative Plan

MENTALLY RETARDED
  Elementary   Partial Segregation   Partial Segregation
  Secondary   Cooperative   Cooperative

MENTALLY DEFICIENT
  Elementary   Segregated   Segregated

CHRONIC MEDICAL PROBLEM
  Elementary   Segregated   Cooperative Plan
  Secondary   Segregated and Cooperative Plan   Cooperative Plan

3. It is recommended that the appointed Special Education leader give further study to the development of greater emphasis on integrating the hard of hearing and blind student in the adjacent elementary schools for portions of the school day.

VI. ARTICULATION

Elementary Age Promotion Policy

Summary

1. State department respondents, specialists, and professors of school administration indicated by a majority of two to one that the following Special Education categories should be included in the "regular" elementary age promotion policy:

   a. Blind
   b. Partial seeing
   c. Hard of hearing
   d. Crippled
   e. Chronic medical problems
   f. Emotionally and/or socially disturbed

2. State department of education respondents and professors of school administration indicated by a majority of two to one that elementary promotion policy for the deaf should be the same as for "regular" pupils. By slightly less than a two to one majority, specialists indicated that the deaf child should be included in the "regular" elementary promotion policy.

3. The majority of the specialists and professors of school administration indicated that the mentally retarded should not be included in the promotion policy used for "regular" pupils. A slight majority of state department of education respondents

indicated preference for including mentally retarded pupils in the promotion policy for "regular" pupils.

4. State department of education respondents, specialists, and professors of school administration indicated by a two to one majority that the mentally deficient should not be included in the promotion policy used for "regular" pupils.

Conclusions and Recommendations

1. It may be concluded that exceptional children should be included in the "regular" elementary age promotion policy with the exception of the mentally retarded and the mentally deficient.

2. A thorough study should be made to determine the degree of flexibility needed in developing a sound age promotion policy. Careful study may conclude that the deaf child will need additional elementary school experience prior to promotion to junior high school. However, if a consistent and planned program of Special Education for grades I through XII is provided, the transition from the elementary level to the junior high school level should allow a similar elementary age promotion policy as now provided for "regular" pupils.

3. It is recommended that grades VII and VIII for crippled children be transferred from the Division of Elementary Education to the Division of Secondary Education. Advantages accrued in the change are as follows:

   a. A larger secondary school enrollment would facilitate and improve teacher assignment to subject areas of personal competency relative to college training and experience.

   b. The grouping of pupils for instructional purposes would be improved with a larger enrollment.

   c. The curriculum could be expanded to include a wider range of subject offerings and strengthen the vocational-occupational training opportunities. At the present time, there is little opportunity for secondary crippled and delicate students to develop skills and competencies in "shop" activities, business education, handicrafts, and homemaking, etc.

d. It would eliminate the possibility of an injured or post-operative junior high school pupil returning to an elementary school for Special Education placement.

e. It would make uniform the present articulation policy of a six year elementary program and a six year secondary program.

f. It would strengthen the educational experience for students terminated from further schooling at sixteen years of age. At the present time, children may be assigned to Widney from an elementary school at age fifteen. If the child is to terminate his education at sixteen, this allows only a one year experience in high school.

g. The Controlling Division publication, *Expenditures Classified by Schools*, October 8, 1959, indicated that the cost per capita would be approximately the same for pupil education in either the elementary schools for the crippled and delicate or Widney.

High School Age Graduation Policy

Summary

1. State department respondents, specialists, and professors of school administration indicated by a majority of two to one that the following Special Education categories should be included in a "regular" high school age graduation policy:

   a. Blind
   b. Partial seeing
   c. Hard of hearing
   d. Crippled
   e. Chronic medical problems
   f. Emotionally and/or socially disturbed

2. Respondents were agreed that the mentally deficient should not be included in a high school age graduation policy. This finding is consistent with respondent recommendation that training of mentally deficient children should not be the responsibility of public schools.

3. State department respondents indicated by a two to one majority that the mentally retarded group should not be included in a "regular" high school age graduation policy. Specialists were evenly divided in response to the item. A majority of professors of school administration recommended that the mentally retarded should be included in the "regular" high school age graduation policy.
4. Specialists were evenly divided in response to indicating whether the deaf should be included in a "regular" high school age graduation policy. Two out of every three state department of education respondents recommended that the deaf student should be included in the "regular" high school age graduation policy. Professors of school administration indicated by a three to one majority that secondary deaf students should be included in the "regular" high school age graduation policy.

Conclusions and Recommendations

1. It may be concluded that all categories of Special Education except the (1) mentally deficient, (2) mentally retarded, and (3) deaf may be included in the regular high school age graduation policy.
2. The present Los Angeles High School District age graduation policy is sufficiently flexible to allow needed educational adjustments and provisions for the exceptional child.

VII. PROFESSIONAL TRAINING

Recommended Professional Training for a Principal of a Special Education School

Summary

1. State department of education respondents and specialists indicated by a majority of more than three to one that a principal of a Special Education school should possess a Special Education Credential.
2. Professors of school administration indicated by a majority of more than two to one that a principal of a Special Education school should possess a Special Education Credential.

Conclusions and Recommendations

1. Principals of Special Education schools should possess a Special Education Credential.
2. The current practice of appointing principals with experience and background in Special Education and who also possess a Special Education Credential should be continued.

Recommended Professional Training for a Principal of a School Containing Special Education Classes

Summary

1. State department of education respondents and professors of school administration indicated by a majority of approximately eight to one that principals of schools containing Special Education classes should have from four to six hours of basic university course work in Special Education.
2. Specialists indicated by a majority of two to one that principals of schools containing Special Education classes should have from four to six hours of basic university course work in Special Education. However, twenty-eight per cent of the specialists indicate that a principal should possess a Special Education Credential.
3. Five per cent of the state department respondents and ten per cent of the professors of school administration indicated that professional college course work in Special Education should not be a prerequisite to assignment to a school containing Special Education classes.

Conclusions and Recommendations

1. Principals of schools containing Special Education classes should have from four to six hours of basic course work in Special Education.
2. It is recommended that whenever possible no more than one (integrated) category of Special Education be placed in an elementary school. Principals of schools containing an integrative class, or classes, should accept the responsibility for obtaining further professional in-service or college training in the area of Special Education assigned to his school.

VIII. ADMINISTRATIVE FRAMEWORK

Recommended Administrative Framework for Special Education Schools

Summary

1. Data received from state department respondents and specialists found a considerable spread in responses among the four administrative framework plan categories. No single plan received more than a forty per cent positive response. Professors of school administration, however, gave evidence of favoring one administrative framework plan as determined by a simple majority response.

2. State department respondents and professors of school administration gave highest frequency to the administrative plan whereby the principal of a Special Education school was directly responsible to a District Assistant Superintendent. The same respondents indicated second choice to the plan in which a separate department or division of Special Education is formed for administrative control of Special Education schools.

3. Specialists gave highest frequency to the administrative framework plan whereby the Special Education principal was directly responsible to a separate department or division of Special Education. Second choice was evenly divided in frequency count between direct line relationship with the operational District Superintendent and the plan whereby dual line authority stemmed from both the separate department of Special Education and the operational Assistant Superintendent.

Conclusions and Recommendations

1. Specialists and state department respondents failed to give any one administrative framework plan a majority response. It may be inferred from data received from specialists and state department of education respondents that there is a lack of clear agreement as to the most suitable administrative framework plan for large city school districts.

2. It may be concluded, with qualification, that specialists tend to favor an administrative framework plan whereby the de-

partment or division of Special Education has the entire or shared control and responsibility for Special Education schools.

3. It may be concluded, with qualification, that state department of education respondents tend to favor an administrative framework plan whereby the local District Assistant Superintendent has the entire or shared responsibility for Special Education schools in his district.

4. It may be concluded that professors of school administration recommend, without qualification, that the local District Assistant Superintendent be responsible for Special Education schools in his district.

5. The inconclusive nature of the data received regarding the recommended administrative framework would indicate that the Los Angeles City School District should develop framework consistent to local need and conditions.

Recommended Administrative Framework for Schools Containing Special Education Classes

Summary

1. The majority of specialists favored the administrative framework plan whereby the principal of a school containing Special Education classes would be under the dual control of two superintendents, namely: (1) the local District Assistant Superintendent and, (2) the head of the department or division of Special Education.

2. Professors of school administration were in agreement, as determined by a majority of frequencies, in recommending that the local Assistant Superintendent be responsible for the schools in his district which include Special Education classes.

3. Data received from state department of education respondents found a considerable spread in responses among the four administrative framework plan categories. No single plan received more than a forty-three per cent positive response. However, when the frequency responses for Plan I and II are totalled and compared to the total frequency for Plan III and IV, it becomes evident that the majority of state department

respondents favor "regular" administrative control over schools containing Special Education classes.

Conclusions and Recommendations

1. It may be concluded from an analysis of data that respondents gave clear evidence for the recommendation that partial or full administrative control should be vested in the District Assistant Superintendent relative to schools containing Special Education classes.
2. It is therefore recommended that any change in the administrative framework for the Special Education program recognize the importance of local District Assistant Superintendent control over schools containing Special Education classes.

IX. CITY SCHOOL ADMINISTRATIVE FRAMEWORK

Current Administrative Framework for Special Education Programs in Large City School Districts

Summary

1. In an analysis of line and staff charts received from forty-nine cities, with a population of 200,000 or more, the following forms of administrative framework for the Special Education program are found:

   a. Fifteen city school districts, or thirty-one per cent, were found to have an administrative framework that placed the Special Education leader within the operational division or district. In all instances, the Special Education leader was vested with advisory or staff relationship with schools and personnel involved in educating the exceptional child. Responsibility for Special Education schools, as defined by line and staff authority, was found to be assigned to the District Assistant Superintendent.

   b. Eighteen city school districts, or thirty-six per cent, were found to have an administrative framework that placed the Special Education department in a division other than operational. In all instances, the Special Education leader was vested with advisory or staff relationship with school personnel. Administrative responsibility for Special Education schools and classes was assigned to the District Assistant Superintendent. School districts which placed the department of Special Education in a division other than operational or as a separate entity, tended to favor three types of divisions, namely: (1) Curriculum Branch; (2) Pupil Personnel Services or similar title; and, (3) Guidance.

   c. Sixteen school districts, or thirty-three per cent, were found to grant line authority over schools and classes of Special Education to the Special Education leader.

2. The most frequent rank given to the leader of the Special Education program was found to be "Director."

Conclusions and Recommendations

1. It may be concluded from the data received that there is no one single form of administrative organization currently in operation for the Special Education program in large city school districts throughout the United States.

2. It may be inferred and concluded that the variety of Special Education administrative framework patterns found in large city school systems throughout the United States are a reflection of local district internal needs.

3. Since current administrative patterns vary greatly among the large city school systems, there is sufficient evidence to recommend that the Los Angeles City School District place emphasis on local needs and conditions in the development of an administrative framework for the Special Education program.

X. LARGE CITY SCHOOL SYSTEMS RECOMMENDED FOR PERSONAL VISITATION

Summary

The eight city school systems that received highest frequency of mention by a composite of specialists and state department of education respondents are presented in the following rank order:

   1 Detroit, Michigan
   2 Chicago, Illinois

3 Cincinnati, Ohio
5 New York, New York
5 Newark, New Jersey
5 Cleveland, Ohio
7.5 Pittsburgh, Pennsylvania
7.5 Portland, Oregon

Conclusions and Recommendations

1. For the purpose of this study, specialists and state department of education respondents were classified as experts in the field of Special Education. It is thus assumed that the eight city school districts that received the highest number of frequencies, as determined by a composite of specialists and state department respondents, represent a sampling of the finest Special Education programs in the United States.
2. It is recommended that the eight city school systems receiving highest frequency of mention by a composite of specialists and state department of education respondents be visited by the investigator to determine and observe the current administrative framework.

XI. UNSOLVED DILEMMAS AND PROBLEMS IN THE FIELD OF SPECIAL EDUCATION

Inherent within the program of Special Education are basic problems which represent dilemmas in administering, organizing, and supervising the educational program for exceptional children. If the problem is basically a dilemma in character, choice and decision must be made which, by definition, will result in producing negative factors. Alternative decisions would, in most cases, produce an equal or greater number of frictions or negative factors.

The Dilemma of Integration vs. Segregation

Decisions related to the degree in practice of integration-segregation will be theoretically determined by such factors as: (1) age of pupil; (2) degree of handicap; (3) emotional stability of pupil; (4) facilities available; (5) number of pupils with a similar handicap; (6) degree of emphasis on basic skills vs. social/

emotional adjustment; (7) attitude of teachers and administrators involved in the educational program of the handicapped; (8) type of handicap, etc. Allied to the factors listed above is the parent expectancy of school services that should be rendered.

The need for segregation of selected pupils for specialized educational opportunity is as necessary and as desirable as the need for integrating selected pupils with lesser handicaps into regular classrooms. The problem, or dilemma, is represented by the "gray area" between integration and segregation; e.g. pupils who might, under certain conditions, be placed in either an integrated or segregated educational program depending on the facilities and personnel available. The problem of integration vs. segregation, in many instances, is as much a problem of attitude as of the actual physical condition or disability. Attitude or mental set toward the physical disability may be a greater handicap than the actual physical condition or limitation. Thus, the unsolved problem of integration vs. segregation may be specifically stated as follows:

> To what degree should we integrate or segregate a given category of Special Education to allow maximum educational opportunity while recognizing the physical, emotional, legal, economic, and mental set limitations?

Specialized Services vs. Time-Distance Factor

Concomitant to the problem of integration vs. segregation is the dilemma of specialized services vs. the time-distance factor in transporting pupils. The number of deaf, blind, partially seeing, and crippled pupils necessary to allow specialized services, some degree of pupil homogeneity for instructional purposes, and a sufficient staff to allow group planning and extra curricula activities may necessitate a Special Education school as opposed to classes or centers. However, a Special Education school, in turn, creates a problem of obtaining a sufficient number of pupils in order to maintain the necessary enrollment to justify an extensive education program. Thus, the children who attend a Special Education school in Los Angeles may be transported from wide geographic points. In one case, the longest riding time in the Los

Angeles City School District is one hour and fifty-two minutes (Mary E. Bennett School). Specifically stated is the dilemma:

What is the minimum number of pupils for each given category of Special Education necessary to maintain a strong educational program for a Special Education school or center?

Generalist vs. Specialist

The dilemma of generalist vs. specialist may be observed in two settings.

Auxiliary and instructional personnel may tend to express and over-emphasize the training and experience of their particular discipline. For example, the medical section may tend to limit evaluation and recommendation for pupil classroom placement to physiological limitations. The psychologist or counselor may limit conception of pupil adjustment to the individual child rather than the effect it will have on the individuals comprising a group situation. The "regular" school principal may overemphasize the legal factors, playground problem, teacher morale, and super-vision difficulties. The "regular" classroom teacher may observe the handicapped pupil as a member of a group, placing stress on total group instruction as opposed to an individualized and/or modified educational program for an integrated handicapped pupil. If the handicapped pupil necessitates individual attention or a disproportionate amount of teacher time, question is raised as to the justification of integration on the basis of group welfare. Thus, each discipline; medicine, education, and psychology places stress on different facets of pupil adjustment to educational placement. This tendency is both essential and desirable, but of necessity may create conflicts and communication problems between the various occupational disciplines. This dilemma is observed in any attempt to stressing either integration or segregation.

The second setting in which the dilemma of generalist vs. specialist is observed is in the potential danger of isolation which develops, and to a degree is increased, by a segregated philosophy and program of Special Education. The role of the Special Education program, when isolated, may begin to emphasize the Special Education professional workers' problems instead of the habilitation and adjustment of the children. Also, the lack of perspective and the loss of viewpoint totality results in a potentially narrow view of one specific segment of education. The dilemma may be stated as follows:

To what degree is specialization necessary in educating exceptional children?

Occupational-Vocational Educational Training vs. Academic Educational Training

The degree of emphasis in curriculum orientation toward a broad general academic education as opposed to specific occupational training represents a major unsolved dilemma.

There may be evidence to indicate that the greater the degree of physical or mental handicap, the greater the corresponding pressure for parents to desire occupational-vocational training for the child.

The problem is fundamentally a question of educational philosophy. The degree of specific occupational or vocational training should be answered in terms of the defined purpose and function of the educational program within a given school district. At some point, a hierarchy of functions must be made, acknowledged, and observed as a guide for developing, operating, and evaluating the services rendered.

If vocational training is defined as a program of education organized to prepare the learner for entrance into a particular chosen vocation such as trade, industry, agriculture, etc., it may be said that the Los Angeles City School District is to a degree offering vocational training. However, specific skills within the above described division of labor are not developed to allow narrow specialization such as watch or shoe repairing.

The question, or dilemma, is further developed by asking, what specific skills should be taught? The dilemma may be phrased as follows:

What are the confines, responsibilities, and obligations of the public school, state agencies and institutions, federal programs, and parents regarding the vocational training of a physically or mentally handicapped child?

Line vs. Staff Relationship for the Special Education Program

The dilemma is observed in practice rather than in philosophy. It is generally recognized and accepted that self-determination, responsibility, and success are best secured when children with handicaps live and work in as normal a way as possible. It also follows that the goal of segregated facilities, where necessary, is to habilitate the pupil so as to facilitate and allow return to a regular classroom.

In a large school district where the provision of segregated facilities are necessary, there is a tendency for Special Education personnel to desire, and to a degree actually need, direct leadership. The result tends to create a dilemma between the professed need for line leadership by Special Education personnel, and the philosophically consistent necessity for staff relationship between the Special Education leader and the Special Education school. Stated in another context, should the Special Education program be a program *within* the regular educational program or *separated from* the regular educational program? The dilemma may be stated as follows:

To what degree should the practical need for line leadership supersede the basic philosophy and purpose of the Special Education program?

A Static vs. Dynamic Educational Program

The dilemma of accepting a static or dynamic program may be somewhat academic if a degree of flexibility represents a compromise between the two extremes.

However, once a program is launched, such as adherence to an integrated or segregated program, the program must solidify to become functional and operational. The danger of inconsistency and expediency inherent in flexibility may create more problems than it solves. The problem of static vs. dynamic educational operation is readily seen in the pressures brought about by parental groups. Parents of children with physical handicaps may tend to emotionalize the problem and are thus susceptible to easy answers for cure or benefit. This emotionalizing of the problem is reflected and observed in the pressure groups requesting drastic changes in the present educational program. Since the problem is emotional and physiological, there is a tendency for parents to vacillate and contradict, over a period of time, the basic tenets and beliefs formerly held. Thus, once a program for exceptional children is launched after considerable investigation, there is a tendency for a static condition to develop. Small changes over a period of time may create the danger of developing inconsistencies, and a large change creates an emotional climate endangering the total Special Education program. The problem may be phrased as follows:

To what degree may change be made as needed without developing inconsistencies or parental reactions so as to endanger the entire Special Education program?

XII. SUGGESTED PROBLEMS FOR FURTHER STUDY

The following problems or weaknesses were observed during the field survey of the Special Education program and have not been included in any subsequent sub-report.

Problem of Decentralized Housing for
Special Education Personnel

Ideally it would seem advantageous to place personnel with similar functions and responsibilities in a centralized area. By placing personnel with similar problems and duties together, communication and cooperation could be greatly facilitated and emphasized.

For example, Dr. Carl Etter, Supervisor, has an office located in the Meridian Center Branch. His position and responsibilities in advising handicapped students necessitates use of the central guidance file which is located in the administration building. The need to have access to regular guidance and counseling personnel for communication and joint cooperation is made difficult by separation of offices.

The value of housing the Special Education supervisors in the same office area as the new leader in Special Education would facilitate communication and strengthen functional organization.

Long Range Planning for Selecting
Special Education School Sites

There is considerable need to develop long range plans for selecting school sites for the Special Education program. Site selection will reflect the basic philosophy of the Special Education program.

a. Should school sites be selected to allow Special Education school cluster grouping, thereby allowing greater bus space utilization? (Placing children with different handicaps on the same bus.)
b. Should school sites be geographically placed to minimize the school-home distance from any one section of Los Angeles?
c. Should school sites be selected near or adjacent to regular schools to facilitate integration?
d. Should large centralized schools granting extensive specialized service be recommended, or should smaller, more decentralized schools be recommended?

Possible Overlapping of Duties and Responsibilities

Specific counseling and guidance responsibilities and services should be studied and defined to avoid duplication of duties.

Specific analysis of the services rendered by the general Counseling and Guidance Section, Civilian Rehabilitation Section, Work Experience Section, and the Advisement Service might be advisable in order to eliminate overlapping. For example, the Advisement Service is under the control of the Extension and Higher Education Division, and is currently servicing a considerable number of secondary students.

Need for Additional Supervisory Aid in Schools
for the Crippled and Delicate

The schools for the crippled and delicate tend to serve more of the multiple handicapped pupils than any other segment of Special Education. Children placed in the crippled school who have difficulty in locomotion may also have some degree of hearing or sight loss.

There is need to recognize the instructional problem by allowing additional supervisory aid or formulation of in-service or institute classes.

Problem of Selecting Schools for Integration
of Special Education Pupils

A study should be made to determine the advisability of integrating more than one Special Education category in a given elementary school.

The factors of community reaction, increased staff work-load, and the need for total staff participation in study and planning of educational services gives evidence for limiting a school to one category of Special Education.

Appendix B

PROGRAM FOR THE PREPARATION OF PROFESSIONAL PERSONNEL IN THE EDUCATION OF HANDICAPPED CHILDREN

THE following is a description of one of the programs whereby the Federal Government is assisting the cause of special education. This information is self-explanatory, and typifies the interest of the United States Government in promoting more adequate educational programming for handicapped boys and girls. This is a copy of the entire ten-page bulletin, distributed by the Office of Education to institutions of higher learning, to state education agencies, and to interested individuals. This program was in effect through the 1966-1967 school year and will likely continue in effect, with only minor revisions, through 1967-1968. It is a good program and has been highly effective in promoting the training of individuals who will enter the field of education of handicapped children.

DEPARTMENT OF HEALTH, EDUCATION, AND WELFARE

OFFICE OF EDUCATION
WASHINGTON, D. C. 20202

PROGRAM FOR THE PREPARATION OF PROFESSIONAL PERSONNEL IN THE EDUCATION OF HANDICAPPED CHILDREN

AUTHORIZED UNDER
PUBLIC LAW 85-926 AS AMENDED
BY SECTION 301 OF PUBLIC LAW 88-164

I. Purpose of the Program

Public Law 85-926 as amended by Title III, Section 301 of Public Law 88-164 authorizes the Commissioner of Education to:

A. Assist public or other nonprofit institutions of higher learning in providing training of professional personnel to conduct training of teachers in fields related to education of mentally retarded, hard

197

of hearing, deaf, speech impaired, visually handicapped, seriously emotionally disturbed, crippled, or other health impaired children who by reason thereof require special education (hereinafter referred to as "handicapped children");

B. Assist public or other nonprofit institutions of higher learning in providing professional or advanced training for personnel engaged or preparing to engage in employment as teachers of handicapped children, as supervisors of such teachers, or as speech correctionists or other specialists providing special services for education of such children, or engaged or preparing to engage in research in fields related to education of such children;

C. Assist State education agencies, directly or through grants to public or other nonprofit institutions of higher learning, in the training of personnel engaged or preparing to engage in employment as teachers of handicapped children or as supervisors of such teachers.

II. Types of Grants

A. Senior Year Traineeships

1. *Identification and Length.* Traineeship grants are for full-time senior year undergraduate study for one academic year beginning with the fall quarter, semester or trimester. (Senior year traineeships cannot be awarded for the training of administrators of special education.)

2. *Stipend.* Each traineeship recipient will receive a stipend payment of $1,600. No allowance will be made for dependents.

3. *Support Grant.* For each traineeship awarded, the participating institution or State education agency will receive up to $2,000 to partly support the costs incurred by an institution of higher learning in conducting courses in which traineeship recipients are enrolled. Students, therefore, who are enrolled in the program and who have been awarded traineeships by the participating institution or State education agency may not be charged tuition or fees.

4. *Payment of Traineeships.* The Office of Education will pay a sum of $3,600 ($2,000 support grant and $1,600 stipend) to the participating institution or State education agency for each traineeship awarded.

5. *Continuation of Traineeship Awards.* An award of an undergraduate traineeship may not be made to any individual who has already received such an award under this program or who has received an undergraduate scholarship under the program for training teachers of the deaf (P.L. 87-276).

B. Fellowships

1. *Identification and Length.* Fellowship grants are for full-time graduate study at any graduate level for one full academic year which must be completed within the award period. (Fellowships for the training of administrators of special education will be awarded at the post-master's level only.)

2. *Stipend.* For each fellowship awarded, the participating institution or State education agency shall pay to the recipient of the fellowship the following stipend and allowance for dependents: (Level of study will be determined by the institution consistent with the institution's established policies.)

   a. $2,000 stipend for a fellow at the level of the first graduate year of study in the education of the handicapped

   $2,400 stipend for a fellow at the level of the second graduate year of study in the education of the handicapped

   $2,800 stipend for a fellow at the level of the third graduate year of study in the education of the handicapped

   $2,800 stipend for a fellow at the level of the fourth graduate year of study in the education of the handicapped. (This is a special level of study reserved for those institutions which normally require a fourth year of study to complete degree requirements or for those institutions or State education agencies that can justify a need for a fourth year of study.)

   b. $400 per academic year for each dependent (excluding the fellowship recipient)

   For purposes of payment of dependency allowances, "Dependent" means (1) the wife or children (including stepchildren) under the age of 18 of a male applicant; (2) the children (including stepchildren) under the age of 18 of a female applicant without a spouse, if such children are members of her household; (3) the husband or children (including stepchildren) under the age of 18 of a married female applicant whose income during the preceding year exceeded that of her husband; or (4) an individual who receives more than one-half of his support from the applicant and is either (a) a child (including stepchild) or parent (including stepparent and parent-in-law) of the applicant or (b) a person for whose support the applicant is legally responsible, provided that, if the applicant is married, his or her income during the preceding year exceeded that of his or her spouse.

   If a dependent is acquired during a term, the financial adjustment for the additional dependent will be made at the beginning of the following term. If the loss of a dependent occurs during a term, the financial adjustment for the loss of the dependent will be made at the beginning of the following term. (A semester, quarter, or trimester is considered a term. An appropriate official from the institution will determine the beginning and ending dates of a term. The total award for each dependent cannot exceed $400 for one academic year. The adjustments for acquisition or loss of dependents will be prorated on the basis of the number of terms in an academic year.)

NOTE: An individual may not claim as a dependent a person who is receiving a stipend or an allowance in the nature of subsistence from this or any other program of Federal educational assistance (except loans), and may not claim an individual who is being claimed as a dependent of another person under any program of Federal educational assistance.

3. *Support Grant.* For each fellowship awarded, the participating institution or State education agency will receive up to $2,500 to partly support the costs incurred by an institution of higher learning in conducting courses in which fellowship recipients are enrolled. Students, therefore, who are enrolled in the program and who have been awarded fellowships by the participating institution or State education agency may not be charged tuition or fees.

4. *Payment of Fellowships.* The Office of Education will pay a fixed sum of $5,600 to the participating institution and each State education agency for each fellowship awarded. However, it must be noted that the actual amount paid by the institution or State education agency to the individual will be determined by his year of study and number of dependents.

5. *Continuation of Fellowship Awards.* An individual may be awarded up to a total of four fellowships under this program provided that he qualifies and advances to the next graduate level of study with each award. An individual who had received a graduate scholarship under the program for training teachers of the deaf (P.L. 87-276) will be considered to have received a fellowship under this program (P.L. 85-926 as amended).

C. Full-Time Summer Session Programs (Summer Traineeships)

1. *Identification.* A summer session program for which full-time summer session traineeships may be given is one in which a trainee devotes *full-time* to a sequence of courses designed

specifically for the preparation of professional personnel in that area of the handicapped for which his traineeship is awarded. A full-time summer session program in an institution which *does not* offer a full year program will be considered for an award only under special circumstances. It is strongly recommended that a summer program designed for teacher preparation make adequate provision for practicum experiences throughout the summer session. (Full-time summer session traineeships for the training of administrators of special education will be awarded at the post-master's level only.)

2. *Length.* The length of the program, shall be for the full summer session according to the policies of the institution. Pre-, post- and Inter-sessions are *not* interpreted as full-time summer session.)

3. *Stipend.* Each summer traineeship recipient will receive $75 a week stipend payment. No allowance will be made for dependents.

4. *Support Grant.* For each summer traineeship awarded the institution or State education agency will receive up to $75 a week to partly support the costs incurred by an institution of higher learning in conducting courses in which summer traineeship recipients are enrolled. Students who have been awarded summer traineeships by the participating institution or State education agency, therefore, may not be charged tuition or fees.

D. Special Study Institute Programs (Special Study Institute Traineeships)

1. *Identification.* Special study institutes may be held to achieve the following:

   a. To bring together professional personnel already trained in an area of the handicapped for intensive study of a new development in that area (i.e., a new technique for teaching a specific subject in a particular area of the handicapped, etc.). Such institutes, therefore, would not include conferences, evening courses, extension courses, or general reviews of development in an area of the handicapped. The offering of academic credit is not required.

   b. To bring together other professional personnel (i.e., school psychologists, school social workers), who are engaged in providing special services for the education of handicapped children, to assist them in developing additional knowledge in a specific area of the handicapped.

2. *Length.* A special study institute must be at least three consecutive days in length. Full-time attendance of trainees is required.
3. *Stipend.* Each traineeship recipient for a special study institute will receive $15 a day stipend payment up to $75 a week. No allowance will be made for dependents.
4. *Support Grant.* Program costs will be paid for the operation of a special study institute in accordance with the proposal submitted and as recommended by the Advisory Committee. Therefore, trainees may not be charged for tuition or fees.

E. Program Development Grants (Formerly Stimulation Grants)

Identification and Length. A program development grant is available only to institutions of higher learning and is intended to aid in the development and/or expansion of a program for training professional personnel in a particular area of the handicapped. Such grants will be for an award year and cannot exceed $20,000. An institution may apply only once for the renewal of a program development grant in an area in which a previous program development grant was awarded. Program development grant funds *cannot* be used for building construction or to purchase equipment. An institution applying for a program development grant in an area of the handicapped shall not also apply for fellowships or senior year traineeships in the same area. Requests for program development grants for the training of administrators of special education are only available for a postmaster's level program.

III. Minimum Qualifications of Fellowship, Traineeship, Summer and Special Study Institute Traineeship Candidates

Fellowships, senior traineeships, summer traineeships, and/or special study institute traineeships may be awarded under this program by either an institution of higher learning or a State education agency provided:

A. Institutions of Higher Learning. The recipient is a teacher, supervisor, speech correctionist, or other specialist, or is a person preparing to be a teacher, supervisor, speech correctionist, other specialist providing special services for the education of handicapped children, or is engaged or preparing to engage in research in fields related to education of handicapped children.
B. State Education Agencies. The recipient is a teacher or supervisor, or is a person preparing to be a teacher or supervisor in the education of handicapped children.
C. The recipient is a citizen or national of the United States or is in

the United States for other than a temporary purpose and intends to become a permanent resident thereof;

D. The recipient is able to complete the requirements for the baccalaureate degree in one year if applying for an undergraduate senior traineeship, or has completed his study for a baccalaureate degree or its equivalent if applying for a fellowship;

E. The recipient has at least one year of experience teaching handicapped children in his area of specialization if applying for a fellowship (This qualification applies only to those recipients who are preparing to be supervisors, administrators, and/or college instructors. It does not apply to those first-year graduate fellowship recipients who are preparing to be employed as teachers of the handicapped or research personnel);

F. The recipient has been accepted for enrollment by an institution of higher learning as a full-time graduate or undergraduate (relates only to fellowships and senior traineeships); and

G. The recipient has received no other award under this program during the same award year.

NOTE: A person receiving assistance under P.L. 82-550 as amended (Veterans Readjustment Assistance Act of 1952) or receiving any other direct Federal educational benefit (other than loans under the National Defense Education Act of 1958) may not concurrently receive a fellowship, traineeship, summer traineeship, or special study institute traineeship under this program.

IV. Applications for, and Approval of, Grants to Institutions of Higher Learning and State Education Agencies

A. Institutions of Higher Learning

Institutions of higher learning may make application for grants for fellowships, traineeships, summer traineeships, special study institute traineeships and program development grants on forms provided for that purpose by the Commissioner of Education. Applications requesting grants must be submitted not later than the date or dates announced. Application forms may be obtained from and are to be returned when completed to:

Division of Handicapped Children and Youth
Bureau of Educational Research and Development
U. S. Office of Education
400 Maryland Avenue, SW
Washington, D. C. 20202

The Commissioner of Education, with the advice of an appropriate committee will award grants on the basis of the information submitted on the application form and any supplemental information submitted at the request of the Commissioner. Each institution will be notified of the Commissioner's action with respect to its application.

B. State Education Agencies

Each State education agency will be notified by the Commissioner of Education of the initial amount of funds available for its use in preparing teachers and supervisors in the various areas of the handicapped. The funds initially available to each State will be determined by the Commissioner on the basis of the relative population of the State. In no case will the amount be less than $30,000 or more than $110,000. Upon receipt of the grant-in-aid notification, the State education agency will submit a plan setting forth the purposes for which, and the manner in which, it would utilize all or part of the available funds. The State may include in its plan a proposal to expend funds (but not in excess of 10 per cent of the funds initially available to the State) for the support of one or more professional staff members who are directly responsible for the development and administration of the activities carried out under its plan. Forms may be obtained from and are to be returned when completed to:

Division of Handicapped Children and Youth (State Plans Section)
Bureau of Educational Research and Development
U. S. Office of Education
400 Maryland Avenue, SW
Washington, D. C. 20202

The Commissioner of Education will provide for the review of all State plans. On the basis of the information submitted, the review, and any supplemental information requested, the Commissioner will authorize use of all or part of the funds set aside for a State education agency. Each State education agency will be notified of the Commissioner's action with respect to its plan.

V. Utilization of Grants-in-Aid by Institutions of Higher Learning and State Education Agencies

A. Making Awards for Fellowships and Traineeships

1. *Responsibilities of Grantees—Institutions of Higher Learning.* It is the responsibility of institutions of higher learning to take such steps as are necessary to insure that persons to whom they award fellowships, senior traineeships, summer traineeships, and

special study institute traineeships meet all the applicable conditions of eligibility set forth in these policies and procedures.

2. *Responsibilities of Grantees—State Education Agencies.* It is the responsibility of State education agencies to take such steps as are necessary to insure that:

   a. Persons to whom they award fellowships, senior traineeships, summer traineeships, and special study institute traineeships meet all the applicable conditions of eligibility set forth in these policies and procedures.
   b. Awards of summer and special study institute traineeships are made only for attending programs that meet the conditions set forth in Section II—C & D.
   c. Awards are made only for study at institutions, the quality of whose training in the area of the handicapped in which the award recipient would undergo training, has received general acceptance and whose policies conform to the nondiscrimination provision cited in Section IX.

3. *Procedures for Making Awards for Fellowships and Senior Traineeships.* Upon notification of grant-in-aid grantees may begin making awards. A grantee should make every effort to award fellowships and/or senior traineeships in accordance with the levels of study requested in its application. However, if unable to do so, the grantee should request written permission from the Office of Education before making exceptions.

   Funds for each senior traineeship or fellowship awarded are to be paid from the grant-in-aid in accordance with the amount specified under Section II in these policies and procedures.

   As a guide to making awards, the grantee should look upon the Office of Education award as a group of fellowship grants and/or traineeship grants and not attempt to separate stipend and support funds from the total amount of the award.

   Example: A grantee's application is approved for 2 traineeships, 2 master's degree level fellowships and 2 postmaster's degree level fellowships in the area of the visually handicapped.

Total Office of Education Award $29,600
Grantee's 1st award:
   Master's degree fellowship, 2 dependents, plus
      support allowance .... –5,300
   Remaining funds $24,300
Grantee's 2nd award:

Master's degree fellowship, no dependents, plus
support allowance .... –4,500

Remaining funds $19,800

Grantee's 3rd award:

Post-Master's degree fellowship, 2nd year, 3 dependents, plus support allowance .... –6,100

Remaining funds $13,700

Grantee's 4th award:

Post-Master's degree fellowship, 3rd year, 1 dependent, plus support allowance .... –5,700

Remaining funds .... $ 8,000

Grantee's 5th award:

Traineeship plus support allowance .... –3,600

Remaining funds .... $ 4,400

Grantee's 6th award:

Traineeship plus support allowance .... –3,600

Remaining funds .... $ 800

The Office of Education recognizes that in some cases, due to
a combination of unusually high number of dependents and advanced levels of graduate study, the funds made available for
these purposes, with respect to fellowships, might prove insufficient to make the required payments. In such cases the grantee
may not be able to make as many awards as anticipated since the
Office of Education will not be able to provide any additional
funds. All senior traineeships awarded must be for full-time study
for one academic year beginning with the fall semester or quarter.
Fellowship grants are for full-time graduate study at any graduate
level for one full academic year which must be completed within
the award period.

In many cases, as in the example above, funds may remain after
the anticipated awards have been made. Before considering ways
to utilize remaining funds, the grantee would first insure that sufficient funds are available to make payments of allowances for
fellowship recipients who might acquire an additional dependent
during the academic year. In all instances a grantee must pay a
recipient the full stipend (including dependency allowances)
commensurate with his level of study. Several possibilities may be
considered for the utilization of remaining funds.

a. It is entirely possible that an additional senior year traineeship or fellowship could be awarded by the grantee.

b. It is permissible for institutions to pay the difference between the amount a recipient must be paid and the amount
   available from the Office of Education. As in the above

example, after awarding the fellowships and traineeships $800 remain. The institution may add $800 to this amount and award another traineeship. In so doing the grantee must also assume all the supporting costs for the recipient since there can be no tuition or fees charged.

    c. Other possibilities for the utilization of remaining funds are suggested in Section V—B—Transfer of Funds.

B. Transfer of Funds

Funds may be transferred from grants made available for (1) senior traineeships, (2) master's degree level fellowships, (3) post-master's degree level fellowships, (4) full-time summer session traineeships, and (5) special study institutes. Such transfers are subject to the following limitations:

1. Up to 15% of the funds in each area of the handicapped from one of the above five categories may be transferred without prior approval to any one or combination of the other categories. Any transfer of funds in excess of 15% requires prior approval of the Office of Education.

    Example—Funds remain available in the grant-in-aid for master's fellowships in the area of the mentally retarded, but not enough to support another such award. Funds also remain available in the grant-in-aid for summer traineeships in the area of the visually handicapped. The funds available for the summer traineeships may be transferred to make up the difference for another master's level fellowship in the area of the mentally retarded provided that not more than 15% of the grant-in-aid for full-time summer traineeships in the area of the visually handicapped has been transferred.

2. Funds may be transferred only between *approved* areas of the handicapped and between *approved* categories.

    Example—A grant-in-aid has been awarded to an institution for senior year traineeships, master's level fellowships and summer traineeships in each of the areas of the emotionally distributed and the visually handicapped. The grantee shall limit transfers of funds to the three categories and two areas of the handicapped included in the award.

C. Payment of Funds

Payment of funds to support the grants will be made by the Office of Education in accordance with instructions contained in the *Grant Award Document*. Upon receipt of Federal funds, the participating institution or State education agency is to make stipend payments to students. These payments may be made more frequently than once each semester, trimester, or quarter and is recommended; however, the full amount of each stipend must be paid by check to the student without offset or deduction. The stipend and dependency allowance paid to students is not subject to Federal income tax.

D. Responsibility for Funds

Institutions and State education agencies participating in the program are responsible for administering the funds paid to them in accordance with the purpose for which the grants were made. Each institution or State education agency shall designate its chief Financial Officer (Business Officer, Comptroller, Treasurer, etc.) as the official responsible for receiving, disbursing, accounting for, and reporting the expenditure of all funds pertaining to the program.

Funds not expended or not utilized in accordance with these policies and procedures are considered overpayments. The grantee will refund the amount of the overpayment by check payable to the Office of Education. The grantee is responsible for collecting overpayments from award recipients.

E. Withdrawal of Award Recipients

1. *Fellowship and Senior Year Traineeship Stipend.* A recipient who withdraws prior to the end of an academic year is entitled to only that portion of the stipend plus dependency allowance, prorated on a monthly basis per academic year, up to and including the month of withdrawal. An appropriate official from the institution will determine the number of months in the academic year and prorate the funds to be paid.

2. *Summer and Special Study Institute Traineeship Stipend.*
   a. A summer traineeship recipient who withdraws prior to completing the requirements of a full-time summer session program is entitled to only the authorized stipend payment up to and including the week of his withdrawal.
   b. A special study institute traineeship recipient who withdraws prior to completing the requirements of a special study institute is entitled to only the authorized stipend payment up to and including the day of his withdrawal.

VI. Part-Time Work

A fellow is expected to devote full time to required study or research during an academic year.

Exception may be made for post-master's fellows accepting part-time employment by their graduate institutions for the purpose of research or teaching related to their fields of study and degree objectives. Such employment, however, may not interfere with a student's maintenance of good standing in a full-time course of study. A fellow may not teach more than one course per academic year or engage in research or clinical practice for more than the equivalent time for one course.

Institutions are expected to compensate fellows for such services at the same rate they compensate other graduate students who perform comparable services.

VII. Period of Grants

Awards may be used only for programs that commence and end during the award year. The award year is September 1 through August 31.

VIII. Records and Reports

A. Information on Fellowship, Traineeship or Summer and Special Study Institute Traineeship Recipients
On a form to be supplied by the Office of Education, the institution or State education agency will submit such information as is called for with respect to each enrolled fellow or trainee.

B. Records Substantiating Payments
Institutions of higher learning or State education agencies entitled to payment under this program shall keep accessible and intact all records necessary to support claims for expenditures including stipend and dependency payments:

1. For three years after the close of the award year to which such records relate; or
2. Until they are notified that such records are not needed for program administration review; or
3. Until they are notified of the completion of the Office of Education's fiscal audit.

C. Financial Statement and Other Reports

Each State education agency and each public or other nonprofit institution of higher learning which receives a grant under this program shall submit at the end of the award year a report to the Commissioner of Education on a form to be provided by the Office of Education. Such report shall include a financial statement showing how the funds granted under this program were expended. In addition, the institution or State education agency shall make such other reports relevant to the administration of the approved program as the Commissioner may from time-to-time require.

IX. Discrimination

In the expenditure of Federal funds and in the administration of this program there shall be no discrimination because of race, color, religion, or national origin. The program will also be subject to such applicable regulations under the Civil Rights Act of 1964 (P.L. 88-352) as may be approved by the President.

Selected General References

1. BLESSING, K. R.: A survey of public school administrators' attitudes regarding services for trainable children. *Amer J of Ment Defic, 64*:509-19, November, 1959.
2. ———: The function and role of the modern state department in providing special educational services for exceptional youth and children. *Exceptional Child, 26*:395-400-08, April, 1960.
3. BRABNER, G.: Integration and the special class administrator. *Journal of Education, 147*:105-110, October, 1964.
4. CAIN, LEO F.: Special education moves ahead: A comment on the education of teachers. *Exceptional Child, 30*:211-17, January, 1964.
5. CAMPBELL, R. F.: What peculiarities in educational administration make it a special case? In A. W. Halpin (Ed.): *Administrative Theory in Education.* Chicago, U. of Chicago, 1958.
6. CONNOR, L. E.: *Administration of Special Education Programs.* New York, Bureau of Publications; Teachers College, Columbia University, 1961, 123 pages.
7. ———: Preliminaries to a theory of administration for special education. *Exceptional Child, 29*:431-36, 1963.
8. DUNN, L. M.: *Exceptional Children in the Schools.* New York, Holt, Rinehart, & Winston, 1963.
9. ERDMAN, R. L.: *Educable Retarded Children in Elementary Schools: Administration of Special Education in Small School Systems.* Council for Exceptional Children, NEA Publications, 1961.
10. FIELDS, H.: Examinations for the post of director of special education. *Clearing House, 35*:533-37, May, 1961.
11. GRAHAM, R., and ENGEL, A.: Administering the special services for exceptional children. *Forty-Ninth Yearbook, Part II, NSSE,* Chicago, U. of Chicago, pp. 18-37.
12. HOWE, C. E.: Administration. In *Behavioral Research on Exceptional Children.* Kirk and Weiner (Eds.). Council for Exceptional Children, NEA Publication, 1963, chap. 12, pp. 357-364.
13. HUTT, M. L., and GIBBY, R. G.: *The Mentally Retarded Child—De-*

velopment, Education, and Treatment. Boston, Allyn & Bacon, Inc., 1965.

14. JORDAN, T. E.: Conceptual issues in the development of a taxonomy for special education. *Exceptional Child, 28*:7-12, September, 1961.

15. KIRK, S. A.: Administration services and the preparation of teachers. *Educating the Exceptional Children.* Boston, Houghton, 1962, chap. 14, pp. 365-387.

16. KOLSTOE and FREY: *A High School Work-Study Program for Mentally Subnormal Students.* Carbondale, Southern Ill., 1965.

17. LEVINE, SAMUEL A.: A prepared conceptual framework for special education. *Exceptional Child, 28*:83-90, October, 1961.

18. LORD, F. E., and ISENBERG, R. M.: *Cooperative Programs in Special Education.* Council for Exceptional Children and Department of Rural Education, NEA Publications, 1964.

19. MACKIE, R. P., and ENGEL, A. M.: *Directors and Supervisors of Special Education in Local School Systems.* Bulletin No. 13, Office of Education. Washington, D. C.: U. S. Government Printing Office, 1956.

20. McDOWELL, J. B.: The philosophy and objectives of catholic special education. *The National Catholic Education Association Bulletin, 58*:374-381, 1961.

21. MILAZZO, TONY C., and BLESSING, K. R.: The training of directors and supervisors of special education programs. *Exceptional Child, 31*: 129-41, November, 1964.

22. ———, and Tomkins, J. R.: Exceptional children abstracts: administration. *Exceptional Child, 32*:565-568, April, 1966.

23. OUDENNE, W.: A practicum method of training for administrative positions. *Ment Retard, 1*:88-90, 1963.

24. ORR, K. N.: Toward a theory of public school special education. *Teachers College Journal, 35*:181-185, 1964.

25. STRENG, A.: *Children with Impaired Hearing: Administration of Special Education in Small School Systems.* Washington, D. C., NEA, Council for Exceptional Children, 1960, 72 pp.

26. VOELKER, P. H., and MULLEN, F. A.: Organization, administration, and supervision of special education. *Review of Educational Research, 33*:5-19, February, 1963.

27. ———: Administration and supervision of special education programs. In *Education of Exceptional Children and Youth,* Cruickshank, W. M. and Johnson, G. O. (Eds.). Englewood Cliffs, Prentice-Hall, 1958, pp. 648-698.

28. WILLENBERG, E. P.: Organization, administration, and supervision of special education. *Review of Educational Research, 36*:134-150, February, 1966.

29. ———: Administration of special education: aspects of a professional problem. *Exceptional Child, 30*:194-195, 1964.

30. Wisland, M. V., and Vaughan, T. D.: Administration in special education. *Exceptional Child,* 31:87-89, October, 1964.

31. Younie, W. L.: A survey of the administration of educational programs for the institutionalized mentally retarded. *American Journal of Mental Deficiency,* 69:451-461, 1965.

Selected Curriculum References

1. Behrmann, E. H.: Planning the curriculum. *National Catholic Education Association Bulletin,* 57:474-79, 1960.

2. California, Kern County Board of Education: *A Suggested Curriculum Guide for Mentally Retarded Children in Elementary Schools.* Kern County, California, Office of Superintendent of Schools, 1959-1960.

3. California, Kern County Schools: *Suggested Curriculum Guide for Mentally Retarded Children in the Elementary Grades.* Bakersfield, California, Office of County Superintendent of Schools, 1959.

4. California, Los Angeles County School's Office: *Guiding Retarded Children in Today's Schools.* Los Angeles, County Superintendent of Schools, 1961.

5. California, Sacramento City Unified School District: *A Curriculum Guide for Educable Mentally Retarded in the Elementary, Junior, and Senior High Schools.* Sacramento, Unified District, 1957.

6. California, San Diego County Schools: *Suggested Activities for Special Training Classes.* San Diego, Office of the County Superintendent of Schools, 1958.

7. Carriker, W.: *Selected Books for Retarded Readers.* Lincoln, Nebraska State Department of Education, 1957.

8. Colorado State College: *Introduction to Outcomes Charts.* 1967.

9. Douvard, B.: *Teaching Aids and Toys for Handicapped Children.* Council for Exceptional Children, NEA, 1960.

10. Goldstein, H., and Seigle, Dorothy M.: *A Curriculum Guide for Teachers of the Educable Mentally Handicapped.* Series B-e, No. 12, Illinois Department of Public Instruction. Danville, Interstate, 1958.

11. Lauber, Ellyn (Ed.): *Curriculum Materials Guide.* Eau Claire, Wisconsin State University, 1962.

12. Mackie, R. P.: Education of exceptional children: program, progress, problems. *School Life,* 44:10-12, 1962).

13. Massachusetts Department of Education: *A Curriculum Guide for Special Teachers: The Educable Mentally Retarded—Trainable Mentally Retarded.* Boston, State Department of Education, 1957.

14. Massachusetts Department of Education: *The Educable Mentally Retarded—The Trainable Mentally Retarded. A Curriculum Guide for Special Class Teachers.* Boston, 1957.

15. Michigan, Department of Special Education: *Programs for Retarded Children.* Lansing, Department of Special Education, 1960.

16. Michigan, Department of Special Education: *The Michigan Program for the Education of Mentally Handicapped Children.* Lansing, 1958.
17. Michigan, Detroit Public Schools: *Curriculum Guide for Teachers of Mentally Retarded Pupils: Vol. I, Primary Level (7-12); Vol. II, Intermediate Level (12-15), Vol. III, Advanced Level (15-18).* Detroit, Department of Special Education, 1956. (Currently being revised.)
18. Michigan Division of Instruction: *A Curriculum Guide for Teachers of Mentally Retarded Pupils.* Detroit, 1959, Vols. 1, 2, 3.
19. Newark Public Schools: *Learning Experiences for the Educable Mentally Retarded Child: Living and Learning Together (Elementary Level).* Newark, Department of Special Education, Newark Public Schools, 1959.
20. New York City Bureau for Children with Retarded Mental Development: *Resource Materials and Techniques for Use with the Retarded, Reports No. 1-7. Series of Specific Lessons, Teaching Units, and Descriptions of Classroom Activities.* Brooklyn, Board of Education of City of New York, Publication Sales Office, 1956-1961.
21. New York: *Curriculum Resource Materials for Meeting School Retention and Pre-Employment Needs.* New York, Board of Education, 1960-1961.
22. Ohio, Cincinnati Public Schools: *The Slow Learning Program in the Elementary and Secondary Schools.* Cincinnati: Board of Education, 1964. ["Slow Learning" in Ohio is equivalent to EMR in other states.]
23. Oklahoma: *A Guide for Teachers of Educable Mentally Handicapped Children I. Primary II. Intermediate.* Oklahoma City, 1960.
24. Seeley, G. S.: *That More May Learn: Formulation of a Program to Meet Needs of Slow Learners in Grades 4 to 12 of Public Schools of Bay Shore, New York.*
25. SHAWN, B.: *Objectives in Content Area for the Educable Mentally Retarded: Teacher Manual.* Albany, Capital Area School Development Association, State University College of Education, 1960.
26. St. Coletta School: *Arithmetic, Art Education, Crafts, Music, Reading, Social Studies, Physical Education, Language, Arts, Occupations: Monograph Curriculum Series for the Mentally Handicapped.* Milwaukee, Cardinal Stritch College Book Store, 1959-1963.
27. TISDALL, W. J., and MASS, J. W.: Total program for the severely mentally retarded. *Exceptional Child, 28:*357-62, 1962.

Subject Index